Treasury of Christmas Quilting™

Edited by Sandra L. Hatch

HOUSE of
WHITE
BIRCHES

PUBLISHERS
SINCE 1947

Treasury of Christmas Quilting

Editor: Sandra L. Hatch
Associate Editor: Jeanne Stauffer
Technical Artist: Connie Rand
Copy Editor: Cathy Reef

Photography: Nora Elsesser

Production Manager: Vicki Macy
Creative Coordinator: Shaun Venish
Production Artist: Brenda Gallmeyer
Watercolor Illustrations: Vicki Macy
Traffic Coordinator: Sandra Beres
Production Assistants: Carol Dailey, Cheryl Lynch

Publishers: Carl H. Muselman, Arthur K. Muselman
Chief Executive Officer: John Robinson
Marketing Director: Scott Moss
Editorial Director: Vivian Rothe
Production Director: Scott Smith

Printed in the United States of America
First Printing: 1997
Library of Congress Number: 97-71135
ISBN: 882138-21-X

Every effort has been made to ensure the accuracy and completeness of the instructions in this book. However, we cannot be responsible for human error or for the results when using materials other than those specified in the instructions, or for variations in individual work.

Cover quilt: *Plaids for Christmas*, page 123

MERRY CHRISTMAS QUILTING

Quilters love Christmas! It provides the perfect opportunity to make gifts and holiday decorations that are the envy of non-quilters. The care and love sewn in with every stitch is apparent. Whether you make one or many versions of a project, each finished item will be personalized with your own style of workmanship. Enjoy our designers' offerings as you make them your own.

Christmas is my favorite holiday. I do not like the cold weather, the snow and ice and all that winter weather entails, but I do love the Christmas season.

For me the season begins the week of Thanksgiving, although purchasing and making gifts begins long before that. Christmas pattern books and magazines are always ready in early fall so stitchers have time to collect materials and construct projects, either for craft or bazaar sales, personal use or to give as gifts.

At my house, every year adds some new decorations. I now have enough ornaments to decorate three trees; I am lucky enough to have space for them, too! I make, purchase and receive handmade ornaments every year.

I use an antique quilt for a tree skirt for one of my trees, but have quilted ones for the others. I don't like to cover these beauties with gifts, so I leave most of my wrapping until the week before Christmas (that's as good an excuse as any)!

You'll find patterns for several beautiful tree skirts in this book. Turn them into table covers if you don't want to cover them with gifts.

How about special Christmas quilts for the bed during the holiday season? Decorating your bedroom becomes easy when the bed has a Christmas cover!

Doesn't everyone do more baking during the holiday season? If you spend a great deal of time in your kitchen, it should be decorated, too. You'll love the patterns for place mats and other kitchen accessories with a quick and easy theme.

Christmas wearables are popular in the retail stores. Make something different! Appliquéd sweatshirts and vests are among the eye-catching clothing items we share.

Finally, ornaments and other decorative items from folk-art designs to Victorian are offered. From small tree ornaments to wall hangings and more, the flavor of Christmas abounds.

As Thanksgiving approaches this year, I hope to have a number of new quilted items to decorate my home. As you plan your holiday season, consider adding a few quilted items to your home. And why not make gifts for everyone on your gift list? No purchased gift will compare to a special handmade quilted item!

Have a very merry quilted Christmas!

CONTENTS

Wear Your Holiday Spirit

Gifts for the Kitchen

Deck the Halls

Christmas Quilts Great & Small

GIFTS FOR THE KITCHEN

The kitchen is the center of activity during the Christmas season. Homemade cookies and cakes and all those other rich, tasty foods we especially enjoy at Christmas are all fresh from the oven in the kitchen.

Be sure to include this very important room in your holiday decorating! You can make place mats, table runners, towels and more in bright Christmas colors and designs.

Using quick and easy techniques, you can stitch up a few of these festive items while your cookies are baking!

HOMESPUN HOLIDAYS

By Michele Crawford

Cranberry and dark green are as popular for Christmas as the traditional bright red and green. This kitchen ensemble has a homespun flavor when made using contemporary Christmas fabrics in these darker shades.

Decorating for the holidays is fun. This versatile kitchen set includes a table runner, napkins, place mat, apron and tea cozy.

Project Specifications
Skill Level: Easy
Block Size: 8" x 8"
Table Runner Size: 12" x 32"
Napkin Size: 18" x 18"
Tea Cozy Size: 8" x 15 1/2"
Place Mat Size: 12" x 18"

Homespun Holiday
8" x 8" Block

Materials
For 1 Each Table Runner, Tea
Cozy, Napkin, Place Mat and Apron
- 2 1/4 yards holiday mini-patchwork print
- 1/3 yard beige allover print
- 1/3 yard green check
- 1/2 yard cranberry solid
- 1/2 yard red-and-green gingham check
- 1/4 yard Osnaburg fabric
- 1 1/8 yards fleece
- 1/4 yard fusible transfer web
- 1 spool each cranberry, forest green and ecru all-purpose thread
- 1 spool ecru cotton quilting thread
- 1/2" birch button
- Basic sewing supplies, rotary cutter, ruler and cutting mat

Instructions
Note: *A 1/4" seam allowance is included in all measurements given. Sew pieces with right sides together and raw edges even using matching thread. Press seam allowances toward the darkest fabric.*

Step 1. To complete the six blocks needed to construct the projects as shown cut the following: 24 squares cranberry solid 2 7/8" x 2 7/8"—cut each square on the diagonal once to make 48 C triangles; 24 squares Osnaburg 2 7/8" x 2 7/8"—cut each square on the diagonal once to make 48 O triangles; 48 strips 1 1/2" x 2 1/2" beige allover print for P; and 48 strips 1 1/2" x 2 1/2" green check for G.

Step 2. Piece six blocks referring to Figure 1 for piecing sequence.

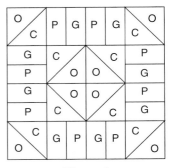

Figure 1
Piece 6 blocks as shown.

TABLE RUNNER
Step 1. Cut four strips 2 1/2" x 8 1/2" and two strips 2 1/2" x 32 1/2" cranberry solid.

Step 2. Join three pieced blocks with the 2 1/2" x 8 1/2" strips referring to Figure 2.

Step 3. Sew 2 1/2" x 32 1/2" strips to the top and bottom of this strip.

Step 4. Cut a backing piece 13" x 33" from mini-

Table Runner
Placement Diagram
12" x 32"

patchwork fabric and the same size piece from the fleece.

Figure 2
Join 3 blocks with 4 strips as shown.

Step 5. Center the fleece on the wrong side of the mini-patchwork and the wrong side of the pieced top on the fleece; pin together.

Step 6. Machine-quilt in the ditch of the border seams. Topstitch around the table runner 1/8" from the edge; trim excess fabric and fleece close to the edge of the table runner.

Step 7. For the binding, cut three strips 1 1/4" by fabric width from beige allover print. Sew the short ends together to make a long strip. Press one long edge under 1/4". Sew the binding around the edges of the table runner, mitering the corners and overlapping the ends. Turn the binding to the back of the table runner. Hand-stitch the binding in place.

Step 8. Fuse the wrong side of a 6" x 17" piece of red-and-green check to the fusible transfer web. Trace three hearts on the paper side; cut out. Peel the paper backing from each heart. Center a heart in the center of each quilt block; fuse in place referring to manufacturer's instructions.

Step 9. Sew a buttonhole stitch around each heart using cotton quilting thread and your sewing machine; sew a decorative stitch 1/2" from the seam of the outside cranberry border.

Place Mat
Placement Diagram
12" x 18"

PLACE MAT

Step 1. Cut two strips 2 1/2" x 8 1/2" and two strips 2 1/2" x 12 1/2" cranberry solid.

Step 2. Sew a 2 1/2" x 8 1/2" strip to each side of one pieced block; press. Sew a 2 1/2" x 12 1/2" strip to the top and bottom of the pieced section; press.

Step 3. Cut a piece of holiday mini-patchwork print

and fleece 13" x 19". Cut two strips 3 1/2" x 12 1/2" mini-patchwork print; sew a strip to each end of the pieced section.

Step 4. Cut two strips 1 1/4" by fabric width beige allover print for binding.

Step 5. Cut a heart from the fused fabric.

Step 6. Finish referring to Steps 5–9 for the table runner.

NAPKIN

Step 1. Cut an 19" x 19" square from mini-patchwork. Press the edges under 1/4" all around. Press under edges 1/4" again and topstitch.

Tea Cozy
Placement Diagram
8" x 15 1/2"

TEA COZY

Step 1. Cut two strips mini-patchwork print 4 1/2" x 8 1/2". Sew a strip to opposite sides of one pieced block. Cut a heart from fused fabric. Center a heart in the center of the quilt block; fuse in place referring to manufacturer's instructions. Sew a buttonhole stitch around heart using cotton quilting thread and your sewing machine.

Step 2. Center and pin the tea cozy pattern on top of the pieced section; cut out. Use the pattern to cut three tea cozies from the mini-patchwork print and two pieces fleece.

Step 3. Center a fleece piece between two fabric tea cozies wrong sides together; pin. Topstitch; repeat with other tea cozy sections.

Step 4. Cut 1 1/4" bias strips from red-and-green check fabric to equal 66" of binding. Sew the short ends together to make one strip.

Step 5. Sew the binding along the straight edge of each tea cozy section. Fold the binding to the back of each tea cozy section; hand-stitch in place.

Step 6. Pin both tea cozy sections together; topstitch. Sew the binding around the curved section of the tea cozy shapes, turning each end under 1/4". Fold the binding to the back and hand-stitch in place.

Step 7. Cut a 1 1/4" x 9" piece red-and-green check. Press each long edge under 1/4"; fold in half and topstitch. Make a loop and sew button through the crossed section of the loop; sew the loop to the top of tea cozy.

Heart
Cut 6 red-and-green check

Tea Cozy
Cut 3 mini-patchwork print & 2 fleece

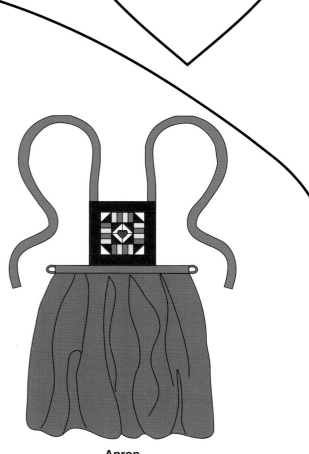

Apron
Placement Diagram

APRON

Step 1. Follow Steps 1 and 2 for place mat to border one quilt block for apron bib.

Step 2. Cut the following: 24 1/2" by fabric width strip mini-patchwork print for skirt; two strips 3" by fabric width green check for straps; two strips green check 1 3/4" x 22" for waistband; two strips green check 1 1/4" x 2 1/2" for tie loops; one 12 1/2" x 12 1/2" square mini-patchwork print for apron bib back; and a 12 1/2" x 12 1/2" square fleece.

Step 3. Fold each strap strip in half lengthwise, right sides together; sew together along long raw edge and one end. Trim corners.

Step 4. Turn right side out; press. With raw edges even, pin raw edge of each strap on opposite edges of one side (top) of apron bib, placing each 1/4" in from side edge; baste in place.

Step 5. Place the apron bib back and front pieces right sides together with straps between; sew around three sides, leaving bottom edge open. Trim corners; turn right side out and press.

Step 6. Cut a heart from fused fabric. Center and fuse to bib front referring to the Placement Diagram. Follow Step 9 in the table runner instructions to stitch the heart and border strips using decorative stitches.

Step 7. Center and pin the raw edge of the apron bib on the front waistband strip; stitch. For the tie loops, fold and stitch the pieces as for the tea cozy loop; make a loop with each piece. Allowing 1/4" seam, pin one loop to each end of the front waistband with raw edges even; stitch to hold. With right sides together and raw edges even, sandwich bib front and back waistband; sew strips together along the short ends and apron bib side. Turn and press.

Step 8. For the skirt, press the short sides under 1/4"; press under 1/4" again and topstitch. For the hem, press the bottom raw edge under 1/4"; press under 1" and topstitch.

Step 9. Gather and pin raw edge of the skirt to the bottom edge of the front waistband with right sides together and raw edges even; stitch. Turn the back waistband raw edge under 1/4"; hand-stitch to wrong side of skirt to finish.

SANTA PLACE MAT, NAPKIN & BREAD COVER

By Angie Wilhite

Santa lovers will want to add this kitchen set to their Christmas decorating scheme.

Use easy machine-appliqué techniques to create this festive kitchen set. This Santa design can be used on a number of other projects including wall hangings and clothing. Purchase a plain apron and appliqué the same design to the front to create more matching kitchen pieces. The possibilities are as endless as your imagination.

Project Specifications
Skill Level: Easy
Place Mat Size: 12" x 18"
Napkin Size: 12" x 12"
Bread Cover Size: 12" x 12"

Napkin
Placement Diagram
12" x 12"

Bread Cover
Placement Diagram
12" x 12"

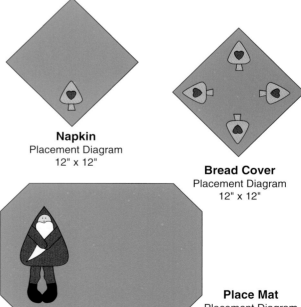

Place Mat
Placement Diagram
12" x 18"

Materials

For 1 Place Mat, 1 Napkin and 1 Bread Cover

- 1 hunter green place mat 12" x 18"
- 2 hunter green napkins 12" x 12"
- Scraps tan solid, white-on-white print, maroon print, black solid, tan print and green plaid
- 1/6 yard fusible transfer web
- 1/4 yard fabric stabilizer
- 2" x 2" piece of lightweight fusible interfacing
- 4" x 5" piece of fusible fleece
- 1 spool each all-purpose threads to match fabrics
- Black permanent fabric pen

Instructions

Step 1. Prewash place mat, napkins and appliqué fabrics. Make templates using pattern pieces given.

Step 2. Following manufacturer's instructions, apply fusible interfacing to backside of tan solid for face; apply fusible fleece to back of white-on-white for beard.

Step 3. Following manufacturer's instructions, apply fusible transfer web to backside of appliqué fabrics. Trace Santa and tree patterns on paper side of fabrics; cut out patterns and remove paper backing.

Step 4. Position Santa on left side of place mat, placing pieces in numerical order; fuse in place. Position a tree on the corner of one napkin; fuse in place. Position a tree in each corner of the other napkin; fuse in place for the bread cover. *Note: The pattern lists the number of pieces to cut for one motif only. You will need five tree motifs for all projects shown.*

Step 5. Pin or baste fabric stabilizer to the backsides of the place mat, napkin and bread cover.

Step 6. Satin-stitch around appliquéd shapes, in numerical order, using matching threads; trim threads.

Step 7. Remove fabric stabilizer from backside of each project to finish.

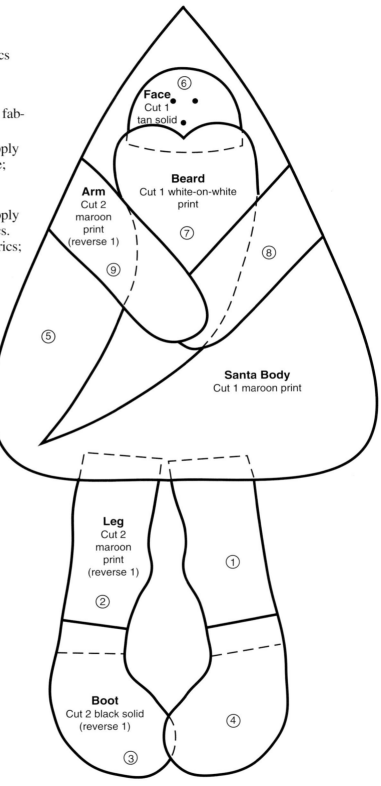

Face
Cut 1
tan solid

Beard
Cut 1 white-on-white
print

Arm
Cut 2
maroon
print
(reverse 1)

Santa Body
Cut 1 maroon print

Tree
Cut 1 green plaid

Heart
Cut 1
maroon print

Tree Trunk
Cut 1 tan print

Leg
Cut 2
maroon
print
(reverse 1)

Boot
Cut 2 black solid
(reverse 1)

SANTA & BAG PLACE MAT & NAPKIN

By Angie Wilhite

Children love to fantasize about what's in Santa's bag for them. This super pattern for place mats and napkins will remind them that Santa will soon be on his way!

This useful place mat and napkin are the perfect announcement that the magical holiday season has begun at your house.

Santa & Bag Place Mat
Placement Diagram
12" x 18"

Santa & Bag Napkin
Placement Diagram
12" x 12"

Project Specifications

Skill Level: Easy
Place Mat Size: 12" x 18"
Napkin Size: 12" x 12"

Materials

For 1 Place Mat and 1 Napkin
- 1 navy place mat 12" x 18"
- 1 navy napkin 12" x 12"
- 5" x 9" red print, 5" x 5" navy check, 5" x 5" white-on-white print and 2" x 2" cream solid
- 1/4 yard fusible transfer web
- 1/4 yard fabric stabilizer
- 5" x 5" piece fusible interfacing
- 5" x 5" piece fusible fleece
- 1 white 1" yo-yo
- 1/4" marbled tan button
- 1 spool each all-purpose threads to match fabrics
- 6" piece 1/4"-wide red ribbon
- Supplies and tools: appliqué scissors, powdered blusher, cotton swab and black permanent fabric pen

Instructions

Step 1. Prewash place mat, napkin and appliqué fabrics. Make templates using pattern pieces given.

Step 2. Following manufacturer's instructions, apply fusible interfacing to the backside of the face and mustache fabric. Apply fusible fleece to the backside of the beard fabric. Apply fusible transfer webbing to the back of all appliqué fabrics.

Step 3. Trace Santa on left side of place mat; fuse in place in numerical order. Position Santa's bag on the corner of napkin; fuse in place.

Step 4. Pin or baste fabric stabilizer to backside of place mat and napkin.

Step 5. Satin-stitch around appliquéd shapes in numerical order using matching threads; trim threads.

Step 6. Remove fabric stabilizer from backside of each project.

Step 7. Dip cotton swab in blusher. Gently make cheeks on Santa's face.

Step 8. Dot eyes with permanent black fabric pen. Sew on button nose.

Step 9. Tie bow with red ribbon; tack ribbon to Santa's bag.

Step 10. Sew white yo-yo to top of Santa's hat to finish.

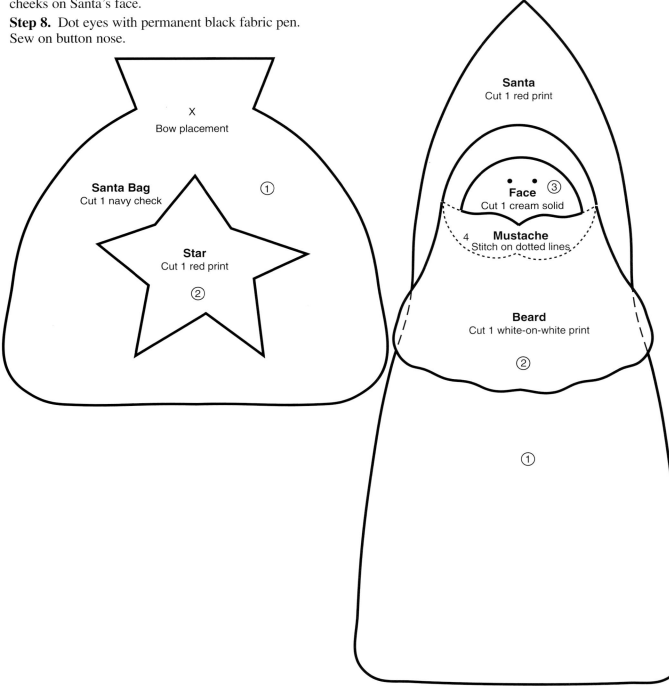

X
Bow placement

Santa Bag
Cut 1 navy check

①

Star
Cut 1 red print

②

Santa
Cut 1 red print

Face
Cut 1 cream solid

③

4

Mustache
Stitch on dotted lines

Beard
Cut 1 white-on-white print

②

①

CHRISTMAS TEA TOWELS

By Angie Wilhite

Place a few of these quick & easy-to-appliqué
towels in the kitchen and each bathroom
to spread the holiday spirit.

It is easier to stitch up four or five of these towels at one time than it is to make only one! Use red-and-white stripe or other Christmas color tea towels to brighten your home wherever a handy touch of color is needed during the holiday season.

Project Specifications
Skill Level: Easy
Towel Size: 16" x 25"

Materials
For 1 Tea Towel
- 1 red-and-white stripe tea towel 16" x 25"
- 1/6 yard green print
- 5" x 5" square red print
- 1/6 yard fusible transfer web
- 1/6 yard fabric stabilizer
- 3 red 1" Christmas print yo-yos
- 1 spool each forest green and red all-purpose threads
- Black permanent fabric pen

Instructions
Step 1. Prewash tea towel and appliqué fabrics. Make templates using pattern pieces given.

Step 2. Following manufacturer's instructions, apply fusible transfer web to backside of appliqué fabrics.

Step 3. Trace tree and heart patterns on paper side of fabrics; cut out patterns and remove paper backing.

Step 4. Position trees and hearts on the lower edge of

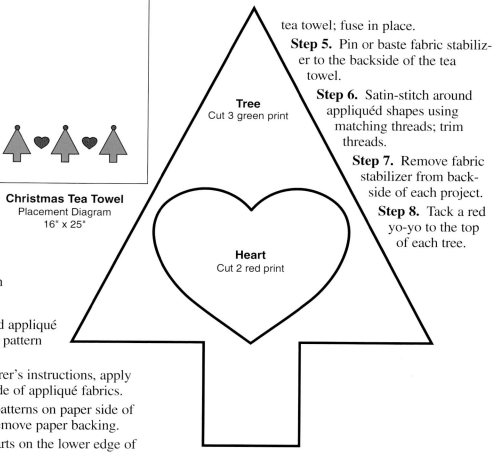

Christmas Tea Towel
Placement Diagram
16" x 25"

tea towel; fuse in place.

Step 5. Pin or baste fabric stabilizer to the backside of the tea towel.

Step 6. Satin-stitch around appliquéd shapes using matching threads; trim threads.

Step 7. Remove fabric stabilizer from backside of each project.

Step 8. Tack a red yo-yo to the top of each tree.

Tree
Cut 3 green print

Heart
Cut 2 red print

CHRISTMAS TREE PLACE MAT & NAPKIN

Project Specifications
Skill Level: Easy
Place Mat Size: 12" x 18"
Napkin Size: 12" x 12"

Materials
For Each Place Mat and Napkin
• 1 red place mat 12" x 18"
• 1 red napkin 12" x 12"
• Scraps green print and tan pin dot
• 1/6 yard fusible transfer web
    • 1/4 yard fabric stabilizer
    • 1/4 yard 1/4"-wide forest green single-face satin ribbon
    • 1/2 yard 3/8"-wide forest green single-face satin ribbon
    • All-purpose thread to match fabrics
    • Supplies and tools: rotary cutter, self-healing mat, clear acrylic ruler and appliqué scissors

Instructions
Step 1. Prewash place mat, napkin and appliqué fabrics. Make templates using pattern pieces given.

Step 2. Following manufacturer's instructions, apply fusible transfer web to backside of appliqué fabrics. Trace tree patterns on paper side of fabrics; cut out.

Step 3. Cut a 1/4-yard x 1/4" strip fusible transfer web and a 1/2-yard x 3/8" strip fusible transfer web using rotary-cutting tools.

Step 4. Apply the 1/4" fusible strip to the backside of the 1/4" green ribbon; repeat with the 3/8" strip on the 3/8" ribbon.

Step 5. Cut the 1/4" ribbon into 2", 2 1/2" and 3" lengths. Cut the 3/8" ribbon into 4", 5 1/2" and 6" lengths; remove paper backing.

Step 6. For napkin, use small tree with 1/4" ribbon. Lay 2" ribbon on lower edge of top triangle; lay 2 1/2" ribbon on lower edge of center triangle; lay 3" ribbon on lower edge of bottom triangle. Fuse in place; trim excess at corners.

Step 7. For place mat, use large tree with 3/8" ribbon. Lay 4" ribbon on lower edge of top triangle; lay 5 1/2" ribbon on lower edge of center triangle; layer 6" ribbon on lower edge of bottom triangle. Fuse; trim excess at corners.

By Angie Wilhite

Sometimes simple things attract the most attention. This tree design uses a triangle to make its shape. How much simpler can it get?

Christmas Tree Napkin
Placement Diagram
12" x 12"

Add a little ribbon and a few appliqué shapes to purchased or self-made place mats and napkins to create a special holiday table setting. Make up a few sets for yourself and some extras to give as gifts.

Christmas Tree Place Mat
Placement Diagram
12" x 18"

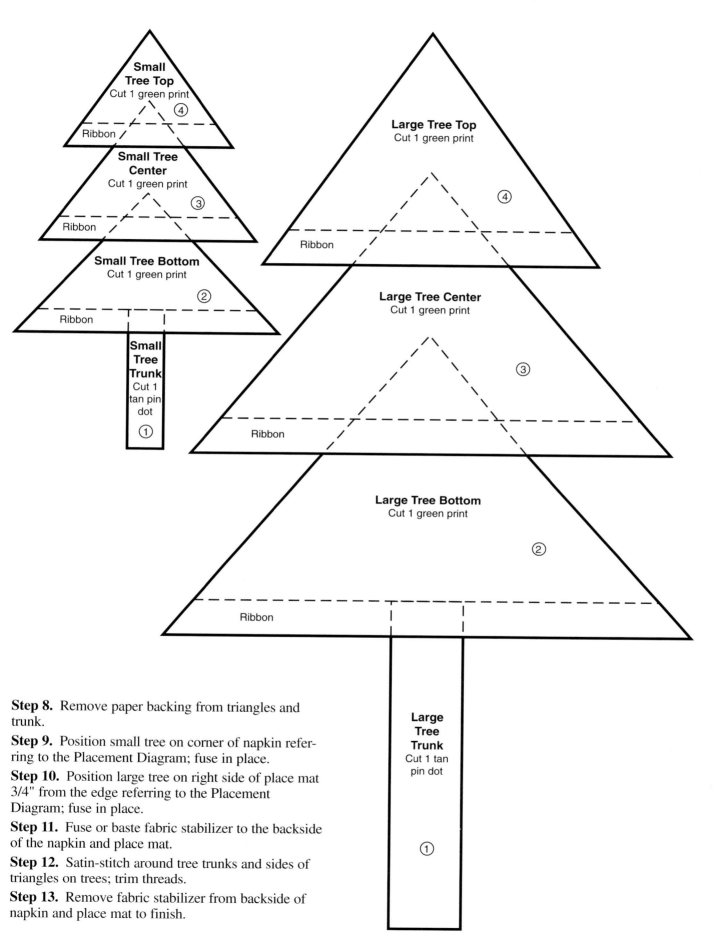

Step 8. Remove paper backing from triangles and trunk.

Step 9. Position small tree on corner of napkin referring to the Placement Diagram; fuse in place.

Step 10. Position large tree on right side of place mat 3/4" from the edge referring to the Placement Diagram; fuse in place.

Step 11. Fuse or baste fabric stabilizer to the backside of the napkin and place mat.

Step 12. Satin-stitch around tree trunks and sides of triangles on trees; trim threads.

Step 13. Remove fabric stabilizer from backside of napkin and place mat to finish.

CHRISTMAS PLACE SETTING

By Anne MacKinnon

Colorful Christmas place mats and napkins provide the perfect opportunity to try out some of those fabulous holiday fabrics you've been admiring in the stores.

Have fun playing with Christmas prints to create these pretty table accents. Make all the place mats the same, or vary the placement of the colors as shown here in the samples. Batting and quilting may be added to give more texture to the place mats, if desired.

Project Specifications
Skill Level: Easy
Place Mat Size: 12" x 16"
Napkin Size: 16" x 16"

Materials
For 4 Place Mats and 4 Napkins
- 1 yard small Christmas print on green background and 2 different prints on white background
- 2 yards small Christmas print on red background
- 1/2 yard Christmas stripe (2"-wide stripe)
- 1 spool matching all-purpose thread

NAPKINS

Step 1. Cut four pieces red-background fabric each measuring 17" square.

Step 2. Turn under edges 1/4"; press.

Step 3. Turn edges under 1/4" again; press.

Step 4. Machine-stitch the folded edges carefully to finish.

PLACE MATS

Step 1. For each place mat, cut one strip 2 1/2" by fabric width from each of the Christmas prints and one strip stripe. *Note: Select a different section of the stripe than will be used for border strips.* Cut each strip into 2 1/2" segments as shown in Figure 1.

Figure 1
Cut each strip into 2 1/2" segments.

Step 2. Referring to Figure 2 and the Color Key, arrange the squares in four rows of six squares each. Join the squares in rows; join the rows to complete Place Mat 1. Press seams.

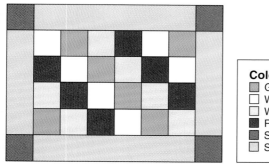

Figure 3
Arrange squares for Place Mat 2 as shown.

Figure 4
Arrange squares for Place Mat 3 as shown.

Color Key
- Green print
- White print #1
- White print #2
- Red/white/green print
- Stripe
- Stripe

Figure 2
Arrange the squares for Place Mat 1 as shown.

Figure 5
Arrange squares for Place Mat 4 as shown.

Step 3. Cut one strip stripe fabric 2 1/2" by fabric width. Cut the strip into two 8 1/2" and two 12 1/2" segments.

Step 4. Sew a 2 1/2" x 8 1/2" segment to each short end of the pieced center; press seams toward strip.

Step 5. Sew a 2 1/2" stripe square segment to each end of the 2 1/2" x 12 1/2" segments referring to Figure 2 for color of the 2 1/2" segment. Sew to the long sides of the pieced center; press seams toward strips.

Step 6. Piece three more place mats referring to

Figures 3, 4 and 5 for placement of 2 1/2" segments.

Step 7. Cut four 12 1/2" x 16 1/2" rectangles from red background print. Place one rectangle on each pieced section, right sides together.

Step 8. Machine-stitch a 1/4" seam all around outside edges, leaving a 4" opening on one side.

Step 9. Turn right side out through opening; hand-stitch the opening closed to finish. Repeat for each place mat; press when finished.

POINSETTIA PLACE MATS

By Barbara A. Clayton

This festive set of holiday place mats with matching center hot pad is the perfect decorative touch for a round table. Place a plain red or green tablecloth underneath the place mats to add a colorful finishing touch to your dining room.

Most purchased place mats are square. If you have a round table, square mats don't enhance the shape of the table. These easy-to-stitch mats are the perfect solution.

Project Specifications
Skill Level: Easy
Place Mat Size: 11 1/4" x 25 1/2"
Hot Pad Size: 13 1/2" circle

Materials
For 4 Place Mats and 1 Hot Pad
- 2 yards white broadcloth
- 8 1/2 yards red print bias tape
- 8 1/2 yards pre-gathered 1"-wide eyelet lace
- Scraps red print, kelly green print and yellow solid
- 1 spool each red, green and white all-purpose thread
- 2 yards fusible transfer webbing
- Batting 36" in diameter
- Supplies and tools: white paper, newsprint or paper at least 36" square, pencil or water-erasable marker and black marker

Making the Pattern
Step 1. Draw a 36" circle on a large piece of paper or newsprint. Fold the circle in fourths and crease; unfold.

Step 2. Draw lines on the fold lines with a pencil. Draw a 13 1/2" circle in the center of the large circle to make the pattern for the hot pad.

Step 3. Cut out one of the fourths of the large circle to create the place mat pattern.

HOT PAD
Step 1. Fold the 2 yards of white in half and cut a 36" circle from the double thickness. Cut circle using paper pattern and four place mat sections from the folded pieces as shown in

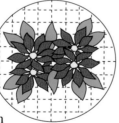

Hot Pad
Placement Diagram
13 1/2" Circle

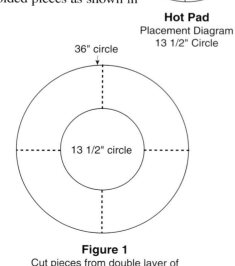

36" circle

13 1/2" circle

Figure 1
Cut pieces from double layer of white fabric as shown.

Figure 1. Set aside the place mat sections. Cut the same pieces from the 36" batting circle.

Step 2. Trace the double poinsettia pattern onto white paper; give the double-flower pattern a 180-degree turn and trace again to make pattern as shown in Figure 2. Trace over the design with black marker. Repeat for a second pattern to use as a guide for placement.

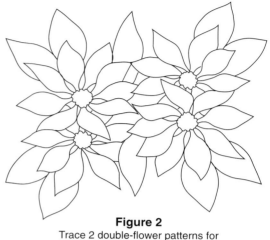

Figure 2
Trace 2 double-flower patterns for hot pad design as shown.

Step 3. Cut one of the traced paper patterns apart to make individual flower petal patterns.

Step 4. Iron fusible transfer webbing onto the backside of red, green and yellow scraps. Trace the petal designs onto the paper side of the red fabric, the leaf designs onto the paper side of the green fabric and the flower center onto the paper side of the yellow fabric; cut out.

Step 5. Place the second uncut drawing under one layer of white background. Using the drawing as a guide for placement, peel paper from behind each shape and iron onto white fabric, layering pieces as necessary. ***Note:*** *The numbers on the drawing indicate order of placement. Some of the pieces from first flower overlay the second flower. Leave some petal edges loose and overlap as necessary when stitching.*

Step 6. Set machine for a wide zigzag stitch. Using matching thread, satin-stitch around each shape twice.

Step 7. Draw diagonal quilting lines about 2" apart across the top, leaving the appliquéd portions out.

Step 8. Place the appliquéd top wrong side together with batting circle. Pin or baste layers together.

Step 9. Lay the red print bias tape right sides together along the edge of the hot pad. Line it up so that you stitch 1/4" from the edge of the tape, but 3/4" from the edge of the hot pad. Fold over beginning raw end of the bias tape 1/2". Stitch all around. When stitching close to beginning end of bias, fold under the raw end edge of ending and overlap with beginning end.

Step 10. Press the tape toward edge. Lay the eyelet lace right sides together on the edge of the binding and hot pad; stitch 1/4" from the edge.

Step 11. Lay backing piece right sides together with hot pad top enclosing lace and bias tape. Stitch along same line of stitching for lace, leaving a 4" opening on one edge. Turn right side out through opening; hand-stitch closed.

Step 12. Quilt by hand or machine on marked lines and around each appliqué shape as desired to finish.

Continued on page 25

Double Poinsettia

WEAR YOUR HOLIDAY SPIRIT

While your friends are wearing purchased Christmas clothing, you can show off your sewing skills with one of these creative designs.

Decorate a purchased sweatshirt or vest in no time at all. If you prefer to invest more time, create your own clothing item to embellish.

Whether you search your scrap bag for Christmas prints or look for brand-new fabrics, the colors of Christmas combine in these easy-to-stitch projects for festive garments.

SLEDDING SANTA SWEATSHIRT

By Angie Wilhite

Poor Santa looks like he is falling off his sled. Appliqué this humorous design to a sweatshirt to wear during the holiday season.

Project Specifications
Skill Level: Easy

Materials
- 1 cream sweatshirt
- 5" x 9" beige-and-red stripes (sled); 5" x 8" green-and-black check; 8" x 8" burgundy print
- Scraps white-on-white print, cream solid, tan print, black solid and tan-and-black check
- All-purpose threads to match fabrics
- 2 cream 1/2" buttons
- 1/4 yard fusible transfer web
- 1/3 yard fabric stabilizer
- 4" x 6" fusible interfacing
- Black permanent fabric pen

Sledding Santa Sweatshirt
Placement Diagram

Instructions
Step 1. Prewash sweatshirt and appliqué fabrics. Prepare templates using pattern pieces given.

Step 2. Apply fusible interfacing to back of face and beard fabric following manufacturer's directions.

Step 3. Apply fusible transfer web to back of all appliqué fabrics following manufacturer's instructions.

Step 4. Trace pattern shapes on paper side of fabric; cut out shapes and remove paper backing.

Step 5. Position shapes on sweatshirt front referring to the photo of the project and the Placement Diagram for arrangement; fuse in place in numerical order.

Step 6. Pin or baste fabric stabilizer to inside front of sweatshirt under fused shapes.

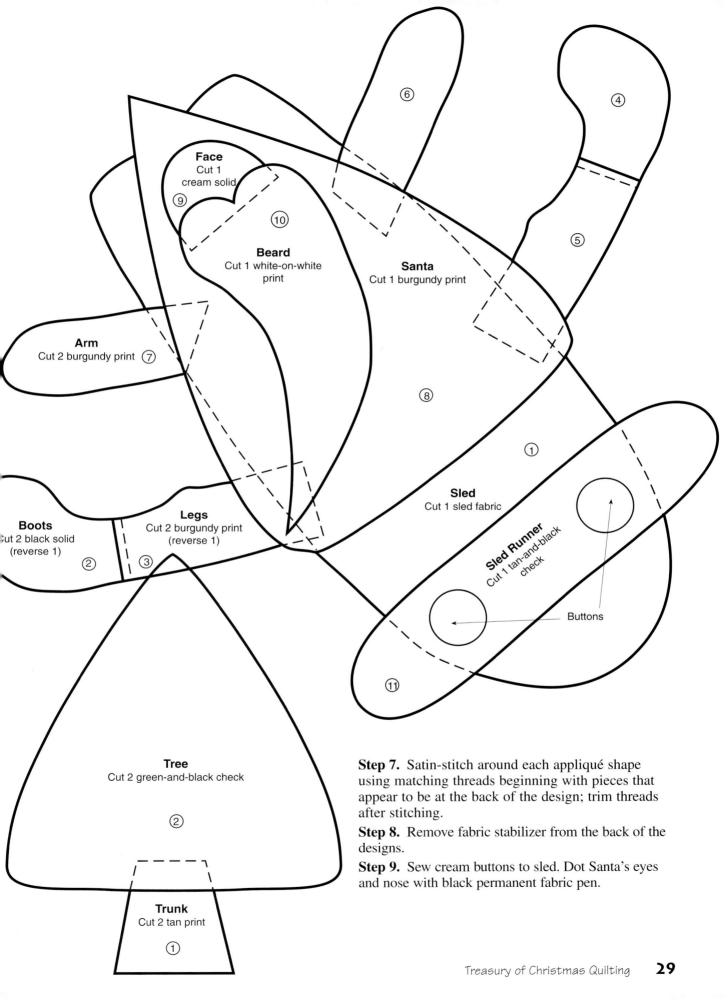

Face
Cut 1 cream solid

⑨

⑩

Beard
Cut 1 white-on-white print

Santa
Cut 1 burgundy print

⑥

④

⑤

⑧

Arm
Cut 2 burgundy print ⑦

Boots
Cut 2 black solid (reverse 1)

②

Legs
Cut 2 burgundy print (reverse 1)

③

Sled
Cut 1 sled fabric

①

Sled Runner
Cut 1 tan-and-black check

Buttons

⑪

Tree
Cut 2 green-and-black check

②

Trunk
Cut 2 tan print

①

Step 7. Satin-stitch around each appliqué shape using matching threads beginning with pieces that appear to be at the back of the design; trim threads after stitching.

Step 8. Remove fabric stabilizer from the back of the designs.

Step 9. Sew cream buttons to sled. Dot Santa's eyes and nose with black permanent fabric pen.

SANTA ON THE MOON SWEATSHIRT

By Angie Wilhite

How can you resist this terrific Santa design? Use quick and easy machine appliqué to transform a simple sweatshirt into an eye-catching Christmas wearable.

Santa lovers will appreciate this pattern. It is shown here appliquéd to a sweatshirt, but it could be used as the design focus of many other items. Use your imagination to create an ensemble using all or part of the design.

Project Specifications
Skill Level: Easy

Materials
- 1 hunter green sweatshirt
- 8" x 9" gold print
- 8" x 8" burgundy print
- Scraps black check, green plaid, cream solid, black solid, and white-on-white and tan prints
- 1/4 yard fusible transfer web
- 1/2 yard fabric stabilizer
- 4" x 6" piece fusible interfacing
- 1/4 yard 1/8"-wide burgundy double-face satin ribbon
- Black permanent fabric pen
- All-purpose thread to match fabrics

Santa on the Moon Sweatshirt
Placement Diagram

Instructions
Step 1. Prewash sweatshirt and appliqué fabrics. Prepare templates using pattern pieces given.

Step 2. Apply fusible interfacing to the back of the face and beard fabrics following manufacturer's instructions.

Step 3. Apply fusible transfer web to the back of all appliqué fabrics following manufacturer's instructions.

Step 4. Trace patterns on paper side of fabrics; cut out patterns and remove paper backing.

Step 5. Position Santa on the moon on sweatshirt front, layering pieces in numerical order. Lay one end of the burgundy ribbon under Santa's left hand. Fuse pieces in place.

Step 6. Pin or baste fabric stabilizer to inside front of sweatshirt.

Step 7. Beginning with pattern pieces that appear to be at the back of the design,

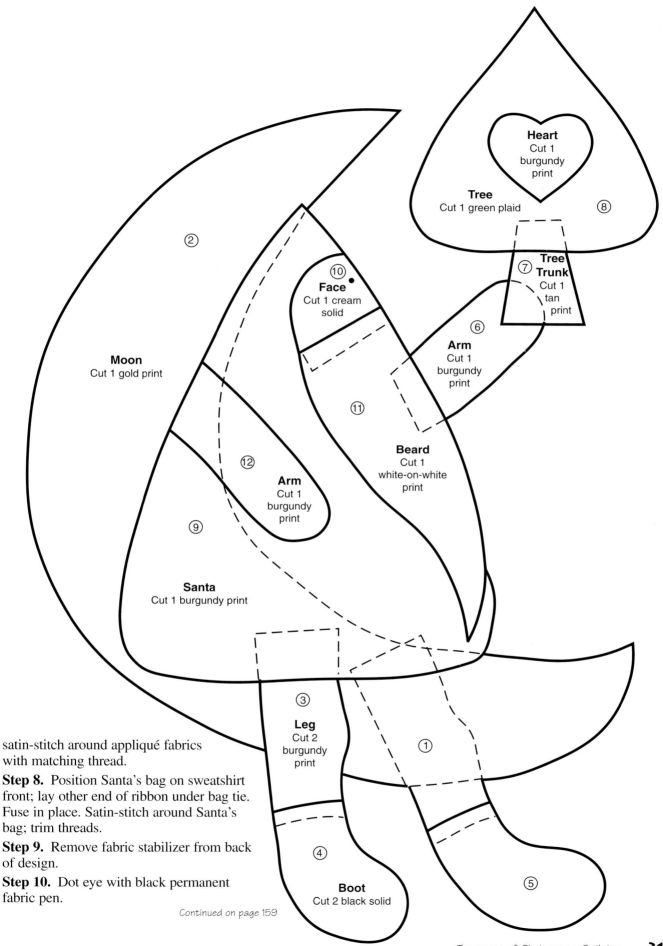

Heart
Cut 1 burgundy print

Tree
Cut 1 green plaid

⑧

⑦ **Tree Trunk**
Cut 1 tan print

② ⑩ **Face**
Cut 1 cream solid

⑥ **Arm**
Cut 1 burgundy print

⑪

Moon
Cut 1 gold print

⑫ **Arm**
Cut 1 burgundy print

Beard
Cut 1 white-on-white print

⑨

Santa
Cut 1 burgundy print

③ **Leg**
Cut 2 burgundy print

①

④ **Boot**
Cut 2 black solid

⑤

satin-stitch around appliqué fabrics with matching thread.

Step 8. Position Santa's bag on sweatshirt front; lay other end of ribbon under bag tie. Fuse in place. Satin-stitch around Santa's bag; trim threads.

Step 9. Remove fabric stabilizer from back of design.

Step 10. Dot eye with black permanent fabric pen.

Continued on page 159

POINSETTIA VEST

By Beth Wheeler

Create a bit of drama in fabric with our comfy quilted vest. We've quilted the front for dimension and left the back free of batting to reduce bulk. Stripe and plaid fabrics in red and white provide a bright background for dancing poinsettias.

Project Specifications
Skill Level: Easy

Materials
- Commercial vest pattern
- Dark-value red-and-white stripe or check cotton fabric according to pattern requirements
- 1/2 yard dark-value red-and-white plaid cotton fabric for borders, plus 1/2 yard for binding
- Light-value stripe fabric for lining
- Poinsettia-print fabric with medium-size, easily isolated blossoms and leaves
- Lightweight fusible sheet
- Feather Touch Cotton quilt batting
- Very fine monofilament thread
- All-purpose white and red thread to match fabrics
- Optional: snap, decorative button or other closure

Project Notes
Do not substitute another cotton batting. The surface of Feather Touch allows stitching directly on the batting; other batts may shred and tear.

Any basic vest pattern may be used. To create the pointed fronts and lapel effect, extend the pattern lines as shown in Figure 1.

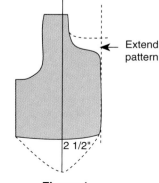

← Extend pattern

2 1/2"

Figure 1
Extend pattern lines on commercial vest pattern as shown.

When choosing a pattern, look for one with few pattern pieces. Beginners should avoid darts and buttonholes.

Vest fronts are cut larger than the pattern to allow for shrinkage during quilting.

Prewash and dry all fabrics, using no fabric softener. Press to remove excess wrinkles.

Instructions
Step 1. Bond fusible sheet to wrong side of poinsettia print.

Step 2. Cut poinsettias and leaves from fabric with sharp scissors, leaving no seam allowances.

Step 3. Cut two vest fronts from batting 1" larger than pattern all around. Cut one left and one right vest front 3" smaller than pattern along front and hemline from dark-value stripe fabric.

Step 4. Place left and right batting fronts on work surface. Center dark-value stripe fronts on batting, as shown in Figure 2; pin in place.

1" extra on these sides

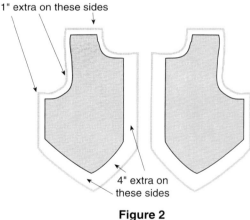

4" extra on these sides

Figure 2
Position dark-value stripe on each vest front batting as shown.

Step 5. Cut two or three 3 1/2" strips plaid fabric. Position along stripe vest fronts as shown in Figure 3, beginning with center front edge, bottom front corner and finally bottom side edge. Allowing 1/4" seam allowance, stitch through all layers with sewing machine threaded with red thread in top and white in bobbin; press.

Step 6. Remove paper backing from poinsettias. Position at least 2" from vest front edges referring to the photo of the project.

Step 7. Fuse in place, following manufacturer's directions.

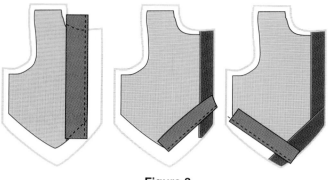

Figure 3
Place plaid strips along vest front edge.

Quilting

Step 1. Drop feed dogs; fit machine with darning or embroidery foot for free-motion quilting. With monofilament thread in machine top and white thread in machine bobbin, stitch around poinsettias and leaves with a zigzag or blind-hem stitch.

Step 2. Stitch on detail lines of flowers for dimension.

Step 3. Echo-quilt around flowers as in Figure 4.

Figure 4
Echo-quilt around flower shapes.

Step 4. Place paper vest pattern on vest fronts; cut to size with scissors.

Step 5. Cut vest back from dark-value stripe fabric. Cut vest back and two fronts from lining fabric.

Construction

Step 1. Stitch lining together along shoulder and side seams with a 5/8" seam allowance; press seams opens.

Step 2. Stitch vest pieces together along shoulder and side seams with a 5/8" seam allowance; press seams open. Reduce bulk in seam allowances by cutting batting away, when possible.

Step 3. Pin vest and lining together, wrong sides facing and matching shoulder seams and points.

Step 4. Stitch around vest armholes and periphery with a 3/4" seam allowance.

Step 5. Trim seam allowance to 1/4" with scissors.

Step 6. Stitch in the ditch through vest and lining along seams from the outside.

Binding

Step 1. Cut one or two 18" squares of binding fabric. Cut diagonally, creating two triangles as shown in Figure 5.

Step 2. With right sides together, sew the two triangles together with 12–14 stitches per inch (Figure 6). Press seam open to reduce bulk later.

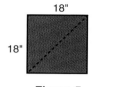

Figure 5
Cut 18" square on the diagonal.

Figure 6
Sew the 2 triangles together as shown.

Step 3. On wrong side of fabric, mark lines every 2 1/2" as shown in Figure 7.

Step 4. Bring short ends together, right sides together, offsetting one line as shown in Figure 8. The piece will now be a tube; it will feel awkward. Press seam open.

Step 5. Begin cutting at point A and follow cutting lines in a spiral fashion until all bias is cut in one continuous strip referring to Figure 9.

Step 6. Fold binding in half lengthwise, wrong sides together; press with iron.

Step 7. Position raw edges of binding along raw edge of vest on right side; pin. Stitch with a 3/8" seam allowance.

Step 8. Fold binding to vest inside, encasing raw edges; stitch in place by hand.

Step 9. Bind armholes in similar manner.

Finishing

Step 1. Fold lapels back, as in photo, exposing lining fabric.

Step 2. Press; tack in place with hand-sewing needle and thread.

Step 3. Stitch a snap, decorative button or other closure just below lapels, if desired.

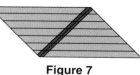

Figure 7
Mark lines on back of the fabric every 2 1/2".

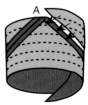

Figure 8
Offset the strips, line up drawn lines and pin together to make a tube.

Figure 9
Cut along marked lines to make bias binding in 1 continuous strip.

TREE SANTA SWEATSHIRT

By Angie Wilhite

You can be a walking Christmas tree when you wear this irresistible Santa sweatshirt.

Project Specifications
Skill Level: Easy

Materials
- Hunter green sweatshirt
- 1/4 yard red solid
- 8" x 8" white felt
- 6" x 6" cream solid
- 2" x 3" tan solid
- 1/6 yard fusible transfer web
- 1/6 yard fabric stabilizer
- 1/8 yard fusible interfacing
- All-purpose threads to match fabrics
- Black permanent fabric pen

Instructions
Step 1. Prewash sweatshirt and appliqué fabrics. Prepare templates using pattern given.

Step 2. Apply fusible interfacing to back of white felt and cream solid following manufacturer's instructions.

Step 3. Apply fusible transfer web to back of appliqué fabrics following manufacturer's instructions. Trace Santa patterns and tree trunk on paper side of fabrics; cut out shapes and remove paper backing.

Step 4. Position each Santa design on sweatshirt in numerical order referring to the Placement Diagram for positioning of Santas in rows; fuse in place. Fuse tree trunk in place at the base of the Santa designs.

Step 5. Pin or baste fabric stabilizer to inside front of sweatshirt.

Step 6. Satin-stitch around Santa shapes using matching threads; trim threads.

Step 7. Remove fabric stabilizer from the back of the design.

Step 8. Draw eyes on Santa faces using black permanent pen.

Tree Santa
Placement Diagram

Santa Face
Cut 6 cream solid

Beard
Cut 6 white felt

Santa
Cut 6 red solid

Tree Trunk
Cut 1 tan solid

SANTA VEST

By Angie Wilhite

Vests are a favorite fashion item, especially for quilters. Embellish one of yours with this easy-to-stitch Santa design!

This stylized version of Santa shows our favorite Christmas friend with a pointed hat with no white pompon. It is simple to create the design with fabric scraps and machine appliqué.

Project Specifications
Skill Level: Easy

Materials
- Premade denim vest from BagWorks Inc.
- 1/3 yard red solid
- Scraps white check, cream solid and black check
- 6" x 6" piece fusible fleece
- 1/3 yard fusible transfer web
- 1/4 yard fabric stabilizer
- 4" x 4" piece fusible interfacing
- 2 black 1/8" buttons
- All-purpose threads to match fabrics

Instructions
Step 1. Prewash vest and appliqué fabrics. Prepare templates using pattern pieces given.

Step 2. Apply fusible interfacing to the back of the face and fusible fleece to back of beard, hatband and mustache fabrics following manufacturer's instructions.

Step 3. Apply fusible transfer web to the back of all appliqué fabrics following manufacturer's instructions.

Step 4. Trace Santa patterns on paper side of fabrics; cut out patterns and remove paper backing.

Santa Vest
Placement Diagram

Step 5. Position Santa on vest front, layering pieces in numerical order using full-size drawing as a guide for placement; fuse pieces in place.

Step 6. Pin or baste fabric stabilizer to inside front of vest fronts.

Step 7. Beginning with pattern pieces that appear to be at the back of the design, satin-stitch around appliqué fabrics with matching thread; trim threads.

Step 8. Remove fabric stabilizer from back of design.

Step 9. Sew a black button to each Santa face.

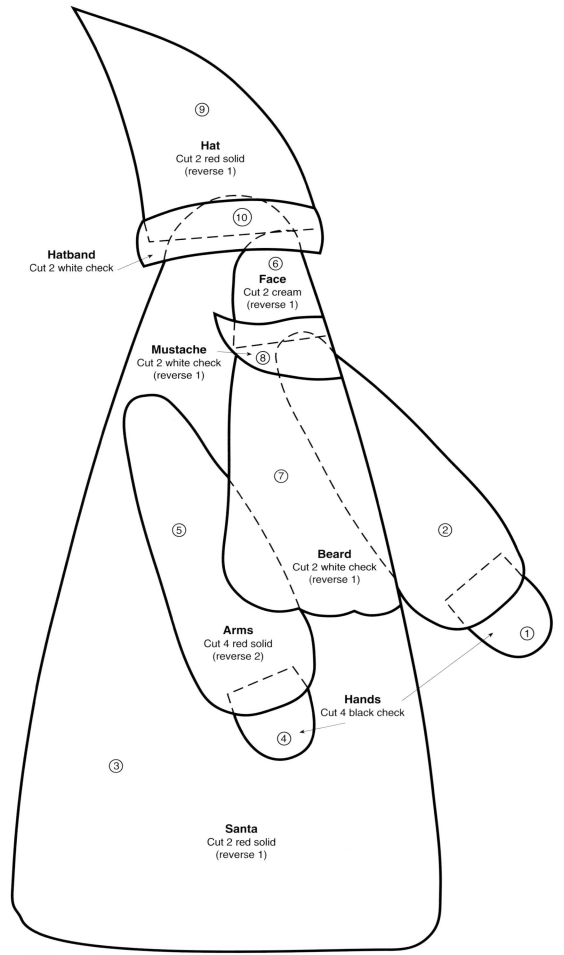

Hat
Cut 2 red solid
(reverse 1)

⑩

Hatband
Cut 2 white check

⑥
Face
Cut 2 cream
(reverse 1)

Mustache
Cut 2 white check
(reverse 1)

⑧

⑦

⑤

②

Beard
Cut 2 white check
(reverse 1)

①

Arms
Cut 4 red solid
(reverse 2)

Hands
Cut 4 black check

④

③

Santa
Cut 2 red solid
(reverse 1)

⑨

FOLK TIE SANTA TOTE BAG

By Angie Wilhite

Santa looks happy in this easy appliqué design. After you have spruced up a tote bag, try this design on the back of a vest or as the center of a small wall hanging.

You may prefer to make your own tote bag rather than using a purchased one. Although instructions are not given for making a tote bag, it is simple to construct the bag without a pattern. If you need instructions, look for a pattern for a simple bag at your local fabric store.

Project Specifications
Skill Level: Easy

Materials
- Denim tote bag 14" x 18" x 4"
- 4" x 6" tan solid
- 1/4 yard white-on-white print
- 8" x 8" red check
- 1/3 yard fusible transfer web
- 1/3 yard fabric stabilizer
- 1/4 yard Pellon fusible fleece
- All-purpose threads to match fabrics
- 1 spool transparent nylon monofilament
- 2 berry solid and 5 Christmas print 1" yo-yos
- Fine-point permanent black fabric pen
- Cotton swab and powdered blusher
- Washable fabric glue
- Fade-out pen

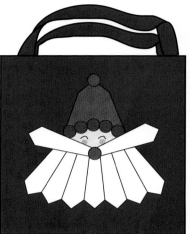

Santa Tote
Placement Diagram

Instructions
Step 1. Prewash the tote bag and appliqué fabrics. Prepare templates using pattern pieces given.

Step 2. Apply fusible fleece to back of beard and mustache fabric following manufacturer's instructions.

Hat
Cut 1 red check

Place line on fold

② ①

Step 3. Apply fusible transfer web to back of all appliqué fabrics following manufacturer's instructions. Trace Santa patterns on paper side of fabrics. Cut out patterns; remove paper backing.

Step 4. Position all Santa patterns in numerical order except mustache on center front of tote bag; fuse in place.

Step 5. Use fade-out pen and ruler to draw lines on beard to stitch.

Step 6. Machine-stitch on lines using transparent nylon monofilament.

Step 7. Position mustache on Santa's face; fuse in place.

Step 8. Pin or baste fabric stabilizer to inside front of tote bag.

Step 9. Satin-stitch around appliqué fabrics in numerical order using matching thread; trim threads.

Step 10. Remove fabric stabilizer from the back of the design.

Step 11. Using fabric glue, glue a berry yo-yo to the top edge of Santa's hat and to the center of the mustache. Glue five red Christmas yo-yos to lower edge of Santa's hat.

Step 12. Draw Santa's eyes with black permanent fabric pen.

Step 13. Dab cotton swab in blusher; make cheeks on Santa's face.

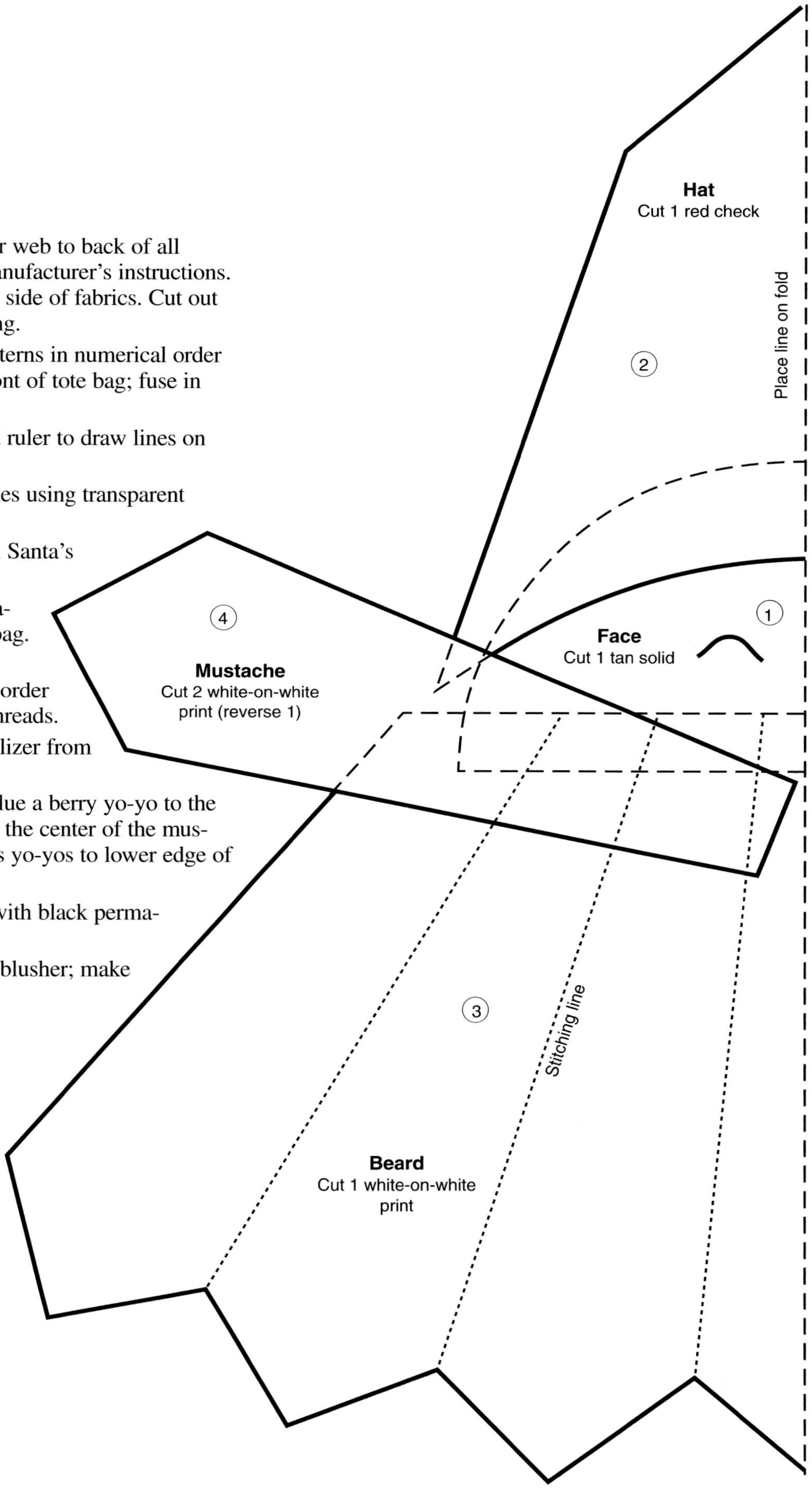

④

Face
Cut 1 tan solid

Mustache
Cut 2 white-on-white print (reverse 1)

③

Stitching line

Beard
Cut 1 white-on-white print

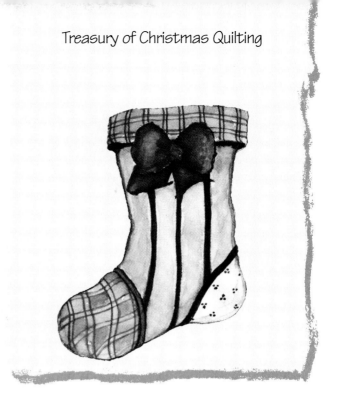

DECK THE HALLS

One of our favorite Christmas carols tells us to "Deck the halls with boughs of holly … 'tis the season to be jolly."

Be creative with fabric and deck the halls of your home with wonderful quilted items. Whether you choose to make something as simple as an ornament or as challenging as a hand-appliquéd tree skirt, your quilted items will add a new dimension to your holiday decorations.

CHRISTMAS GOOSE
TREE SKIRT & STOCKING

By Jodi G. Warner

Combine piecing and appliqué to create this coordinated goose-design ensemble. Christmas colors work together in the Flying Geese design and the appliquéd goose design. You may want to use these two design motifs in creative ways to make other matching Christmas accessories.

If you like lots of detail in your Christmas quilting projects, this ensemble makes a perfect choice for you. Because of the difficulty in construction and all the pieces needed, these are not last-minute projects. Begin early in the fall to allow plenty of time for completion in time for the holidays.

Project Specifications
Skill Level: Advanced
Tree Skirt Size: Approximately 37" x 37"
Stocking Size: Approximately 9" x 17"

Goose Tree Skirt
Placement Diagram
Approximately 37" x 37"

Materials
- 1 1/8 yards beige print (main background)
- 7/8 yard red print (wreath ribbon strips, triangles, center geese square and narrow border)
- 3/4 yard beige ticking stripe (center square, goose body and stocking lining)
- 3/8 yard green with black plaid (outer borders and center geese square)
- 3/8 yard brown with black check (geese triangles, goose neck and wing, center-square border and binding)
- 1/8 yard each 4 green plaids, checks or prints (wreaths)
- Scraps brown mottled (goose wing and tail, geese triangles), brown/beige stripe (geese triangles), red with black check (goose ribbon), black (beak) and cream (head band)
- Thin batting 41" x 41" for skirt; 20" x 20" for stocking
- Backing 1 1/4 yards for skirt; 20" x 20" square for stocking
- 3/4 yard fabric stabilizer
- 3/4 yard light- or medium-weight fusible webbing
- 1 1/4 yards 3/16"-wide poly cording for stocking piping
- 5 flat 1/4" pearl buttons
- All-purpose thread to closely match appliqué fabrics
- 1 spool contrasting color quilting thread

Instructions
Note: The cutting measurements for the patchwork and strips include a 1/4" seam allowance. Patchwork template diagrams show seam lines as dashed lines and cutting lines as solid lines. Appliqué templates are shown as finished size; add a seam allowance when cutting for hand appliqué.

TREE SKIRT

Piecing Wreath Blocks
Step 1. Prepare templates A–K, transferring all guidelines and marks; set B aside. Trace and cut patches as directed on templates, again transferring all guide lines and marks.

Step 2. Cut the following: four beige print strips 4" x 10" for E; four brown with black check strips 1 1/2" x 10" for L; two strips red print 7/8" x 33 3/4" for M; two strips red print 7/8" x 35" for N; two strips green plaid 1 3/4" x 34 1/2" for O; and two strips green plaid 1 3/4" x 37 1/2" for P. ***Note:*** *You may want to wait to cut these strips until you have completed the piecing. If so, measure your finished sections and cut strips the width given by the measured length, adding a seam allowance when cutting.*

Step 3. To complete Wreath blocks, prepare a combination pieced section for use when cutting B patches as follows: one 5" x 13" strip from each of the four green wreath fabrics and four 1 1/8" x 13" red print strips. With right sides together, sew a green strip to a red strip along long sides; repeat for four strip units; press seams toward the red strip.

Step 4. Turn template B and strip assembly over; align guidelines and seam line; trace and cut eight B patches for each block, transferring large dot to each.

Step 5. Position the first B patch along one edge of A as shown in Figure 1, aligning large dots and B seam line with small dot. Leave 3/4" of seam adjacent to large dot unstitched; stitch remaining portion of the seam; press seam toward B.

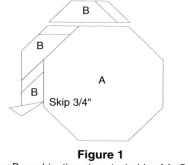

Figure 1
Sew a B combination piece to 1 side of A. Continue adding B pieces to each side as shown.

Step 6. Position second B patch; align similarly. Stitch entire seam length; press seam toward B. Continue to attach remaining six B patches, holding unstitched end out of the way. Reposition unstitched portion; stitch, overlapping several stitches to secure; press seam toward first B.

Step 7. Position and stitch four C triangles to corners; press seam toward B. Designate one edge of each block as bottom; trim off small corner section of both C triangles along that edge as noted on template C.

Step 8. Center and join D triangle to the bottom edge of each block; press seam toward B. Sew an E strip to the top edge of each block; press seam toward the block. Sew the L strip to E; press seam toward L.

Goose Appliqué

Note: Instructions are given for machine satin-stitch appliqué. If preferred, complete appliqué using hand methods by cutting patches with seam allowance, turning exposed edges under to blind-stitch in place.

Step 1. Prepare appliqué templates for four geese using pattern pieces given. Trace templates onto paper side of fusible webbing. Roughly trim shapes around outer edge; trim excess within all but the smallest shapes, leaving approximately 1/4" fusing margin.

Step 2. Use a hot iron to fuse shapes to wrong side of appropriate fabrics; carefully cut out on traced lines and remove paper backing.

Step 3. Arrange the prepared shapes over Wreath block referring to Figure 2 and dotted lines marked on piece A, with head under beak, wing tip under wing, tail under body, ribbon ends under loops, loop ends under knot, etc. Press with iron to fuse in place.

Step 4. Cut section of fabric stabilizer slightly larger than appliqué area. Pin or baste in place against the wrong side of the work directly under appliqué area.

Figure 2
Arrange appliqué shapes over pieced wreath blocks.

Step 5. Machine-appliqué each piece in place, using closely matching thread in upper and bobbin feeds with a medium-width machine zigzag stitch to overcast all exposed appliqué areas. ***Note:*** *Try to complete stitching in best order so that previously stitched ends can be caught by subsequent stitching. When this is not possible, lock stitching at the beginning and end by straight-stitching two or three times in place and pulling thread ends to underside of work. Practice manipulating appliqué area so stitching is uniform with smooth curves and consistent straight lines.*

Step 6. When appliqué is complete, remove basting and tear away stabilizer along stitching lines around and within all appliqués.

Ducks & Geese Block Sections

Step 1. Cut 12 red print squares 1 3/4" x 1 3/4" and 24 beige print squares 1 3/4" x 1 3/4".

Step 2. Prepare half-square triangles by pressing a diagonal crease in red print squares with wrong sides together. Open the red print squares; lay each right sides together exactly over beige print squares. Stitch on the creased line; press seam toward red squares;

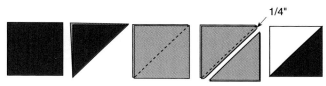

Figure 3
Fold square to make crease: place on top of second square with right sides together. Sew on crease line; trim excess on 1 side to 1/4".

trim away excess beige and red corners beyond the seam, leaving a 1/4" seam allowance as shown in Figure 3.

Step 3. Arrange pieced units side by side in rows with remaining beige print squares for each of the four blocks as shown in Figure 4; press seams toward red print. Join the rows, aligning seams; press seams toward red print.

Step 4. Lay one F piece over triangle assembly, with right sides together and right-angled corners aligned. Stitch long diagonal edge seam; trim away excess beige corners as marked by dotted line in Figure 4. Press seam toward red.

Step 5. Sew one G and then H to each unit as shown in Figure 5. Stitch long edge of the K strip to each G-H edge; press seam toward K.

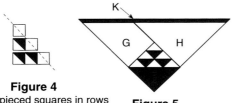

Figure 4
Arrange pieced squares in rows to make units as shown.

Figure 5
Sew G and H to the units; add K.

Flying Geese Panel

Step 1. Cut the following: 96 squares beige print 1 1/2" x 1 1/2"; 16 brown mottled rectangles 1 1/2" x 2 1/2"; 16 brown/beige stripe rectangles 1 1/2" x 2 1/2"; 16 brown/black check rectangles 1 1/2" x 2 1/2"; four red squares 2 1/2" x 2 1/2"; and 16 green/black plaid squares 1 1/2" x 1 1/2".

Step 2. Fold the top corners of all brown rectangles down to align each side edge with bottom edge (creases will intersect at top seam allowance with the area between forming an arrow shape).

Step 3. Align one beige print square over each rectangle end right sides together; stitch in crease; press and trim in similar manner to half-square triangles. Repeat with another beige print square at the opposite end of the rectangle as shown in Figure 6.

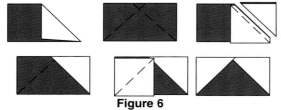

Figure 6
Fold rectangle as shown. Place square right sides together with rectangle; stitch on crease line. Trim away excess after stitching.

Step 4. Referring to Figure 7, join six Flying Geese units together at long edges in repeated alternating order; repeat for eight units. Press seams toward darker side.

Step 5. Lay sections back-to-back in right and left pairs with geese pointing in opposite directions. Sew I to each section as shown in Figure 8.

Figure 7
Join 6 Flying Geese units.

Figure 8
Sew I to 1 end of each Flying Geese section.

Step 6. Press diagonal creases in green plaid squares as in Step 2. Position green squares in two opposite corners of red square; stitch in crease. Press seam toward corners; trim away excess. Repeat for two opposite corners as shown in Figure 9.

Step 7. Sew a Flying Geese section to each side of the pieced square as shown in Figure 10; repeat for four units.

Figure 9
Join wedges as shown. Trim to 1/4" seam allowance.

Figure 10
Join 2 Flying Geese units with pieced unit as shown.

Step 8. Sew a pieced unit to the previously pieced section with K as shown in Figure 11. Press seam toward K.

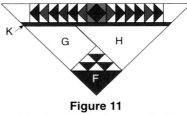

Figure 11
Join pieced Flying Geese unit with previously pieced K unit.

Tree Skirt Assembly

Step 1. For center section, sew L edge of two Wreath blocks to opposite edges of J; press seams toward L.

Step 2. Join each remaining Wreath block between two Flying Geese wedge sections; press seams toward wedge sections. Sew side sections to center section; press seams toward side sections.

Step 3. Stitch one red print M border piece to two opposite sides of center panel; press seams toward M. Stitch red print N border pieces to the remaining sides; press seams toward N.

Step 4. Stitch each green plaid O border piece along the edges of M; press seams toward O. Stitch each green plaid P border piece along the edges of N; press seams toward N.

Finishing

Step 1. Mark center back cutting line diagonally from center circle to outer edge (through corner of circle J and F, etc.). Mark the center J circle onto pieced top (to be cut away later). Mark quilting lines onto skirt top 1 1/4" apart referring to Figure 12.

Step 2. Inside the A octagon, mark a grid 1" apart referring to Figure 12.

Figure 12
Mark quilting lines on each section and center J section as shown.

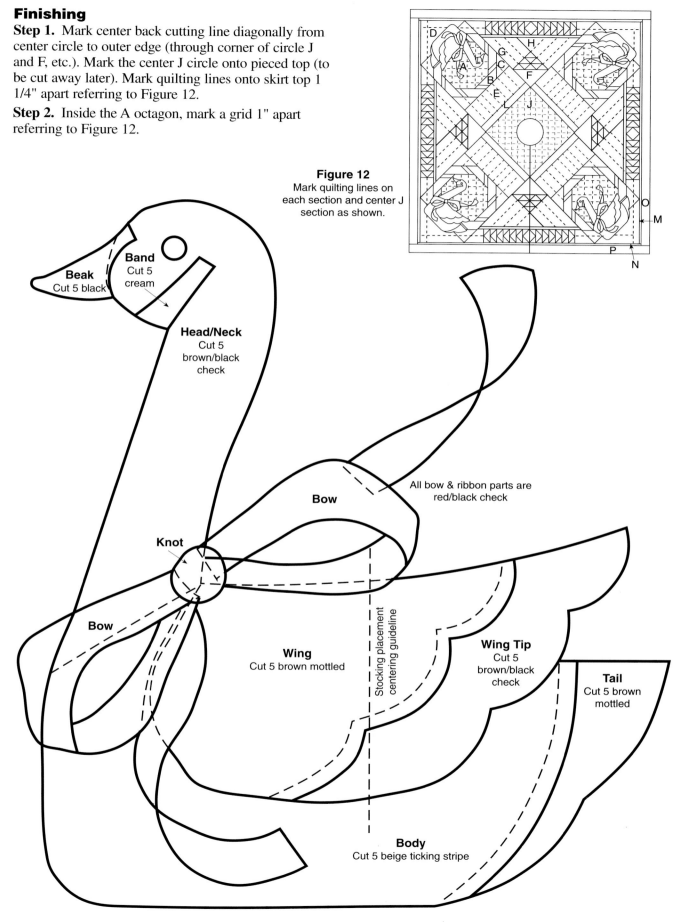

Beak
Cut 5 black

Band
Cut 5 cream

Head/Neck
Cut 5 brown/black check

Bow

All bow & ribbon parts are red/black check

Knot

Bow

Wing
Cut 5 brown mottled

Stocking placement centering guideline

Wing Tip
Cut 5 brown/black check

Tail
Cut 5 brown mottled

Body
Cut 5 beige ticking stripe

Step 3. Cut a backing piece 2" larger than the pieced top all around. Sandwich the batting between the prepared backing piece and the completed skirt top. *Note: The center circle is not cut away until later.*

Step 4. Pin or baste layers together to hold flat. Quilt on marked lines and around all appliqué shapes. *Note: Stiffness created by fusing and machine-appliqué may make quilting more difficult.*

Step 5. When quilting is complete, trim excess batting and backing fabric even with skirt raw edges all around. Cut on marked dividing line; trim 1/4" inside marked center J circle.

Step 6. Cut strips on the bias (diagonal) of brown/black check 1 1/2" wide. Join ends to make one strip 6 1/2 yards long.

Step 7. To prepare 3/8" double-fold binding, lay a 3/4" strip of manila-folder-weight paper down the center of the wrong side of bias, pressing both raw edges over paper. Slide paper along to complete single-fold press of entire length. Align creased edges right side out and press for double-fold bias tape.

Step 8. Cut two 8" lengths for ties; fold one end under; stitch folded ends together. Baste raw edges of ties in place at each center back edge (ties lying toward skirt) at F lower seam line.

Step 9. Cut a 30" length for center circle opening; set aside. Beginning at top center back edge, open remaining binding and lay outer fold line over the 1/4" edge

seam line on right side of skirt, binding flat and inward. Stitch along crease line through all layers, mitering corners. End at left top center back edge; trim ends even with center circle opening edge.

Step 10. Fold remaining creased edge to skirt backside, enclosing raw edges. Align over previous stitching and blind-stitch in place to finish.

Step 11. Measure in approximately 7 1/2" from 30" binding length and attach binding to center opening at that point, stretching around center circle as stitching proceeds. Measure 7 1/2" of remaining binding length past circle; trim excess. Fold 1/4" under at ends; stitch excess bias edges of tie lengths closed. Stitch creased edge within circle to backside.

Step 12. Sew on button in eye position on geese appliqués to finish.

GOOSE STOCKING

Step 1. Cut the following: one beige print 9 1/4" x 10 1/2" for Q; one strip red 1" x 10 1/2" for R; two strips red 1" x 8 1/4" for S; one strip green plaid 2 1/2" x 8 1/4" for T; and one strip green plaid 3 1/2" x 8 1/2" for U.

Step 2. Cut the following for Flying Geese units: 14 beige print squares 1 1/2" x 1 1/2"; three brown/black check rectangles 1 1/2" x 2 1/2"; and two each brown mottle, brown/beige stripe and beige background 1 1/2" x 2 1/2" rectangles. Refer to Steps 2

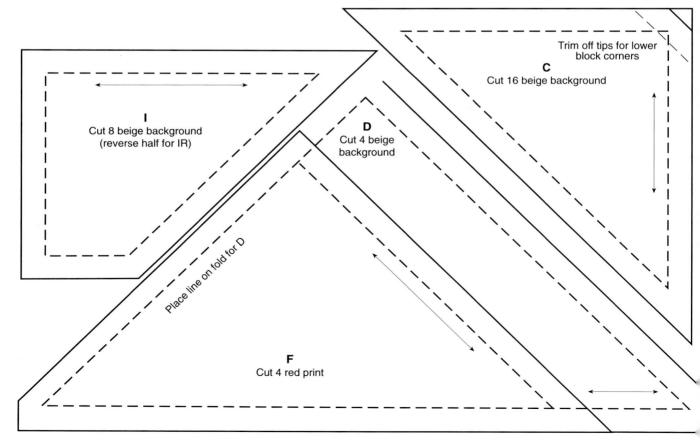

I
Cut 8 beige background
(reverse half for IR)

Trim off tips for lower
block corners

C
Cut 16 beige background

D
Cut 4 beige
background

Place line on fold for D

F
Cut 4 red print

and 3 in Flying Geese section to complete a seven-unit strip. Stitch beige rectangles at each end of the panel. *Note: Trim excess later.*

Step 3. Sew S strips to the top and bottom of the pieced panel referring to Figure 13; press seams toward the S strips.

Figure 13
Stitch pieces for stocking together as shown.

Step 4. Stitch the T cuff piece to the upper S edge and Q to lower edge; press seam toward S.

Step 5. Stitch R to lower edge of Q and U to R (offset U slightly toward stocking front); press seams toward R. Mark vertical center of Q strip.

Step 6. Prepare and appliqué goose design onto Q piece as directed on tree skirt for appliqué, aligning center guideline from diagram on Q center line, leaving equal space above and below goose.

Step 7. Align seam guidelines of stocking pattern over Q seams; transfer stocking outline by aligning seam guide lines on stocking pattern with Q seams. Cut out stocking shape, adding a 1/4" seam allowance.

Step 8. Mark 1" on-point grid lines onto Q around goose appliqué using a water-erasable marker or pencil to mark quilting lines.

Step 9. Divide stocking batting into two 10" x 20" sections; cut two matching lining fabric and one green plaid stocking back sections.

Step 10. Layer one lining piece with batting and stocking front. Quilt on marked lines by hand or machine. Layer stocking back, batting and lining sections; machine- or hand-quilt 1" grid lines.

Step 11. Cut 1"-wide bias strips from red print; join

together to form a 1 1/4-yard length. Enclose cording next to wrong side of bias strip; machine-baste through two fabric layers close to cord thickness (use zipper foot); trim excess seam allowance past stitching to 1/4".

Step 12. With piping pointing inward, position and baste stitching exactly over stocking outline. Taper piping into seam allowance at top opening seam line.

Step 13. Lay stocking front over quilted back, linings out; stitch around following previous basting on outline; lock stitches at opening edges.

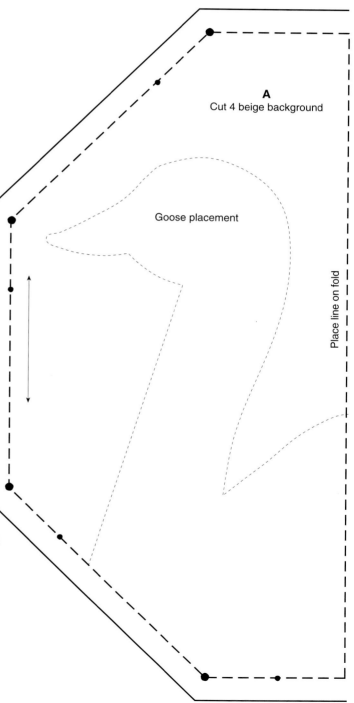

A
Cut 4 beige background

Goose placement

Place line on fold

Step 14. Trim away excess to 1/4"; trim top edges even and overcast raw seam edges. Turn right side out.

Step 15. Prepare a 20" length of 3/8" double-fold bias binding using brown/black check as directed in Step 7 in the Finishing section for tree skirt. From this, cut a 4 1/2" piece for loop; stitch folded edges together.

Step 16. Place loop ends together; machine-baste over seam at upper right side of stocking opening, loop facing downward. Apply binding to opening edge, beginning at center back. Fold one end under and overlap other end when they meet.

Step 17. Sew on button in eye position to finish.

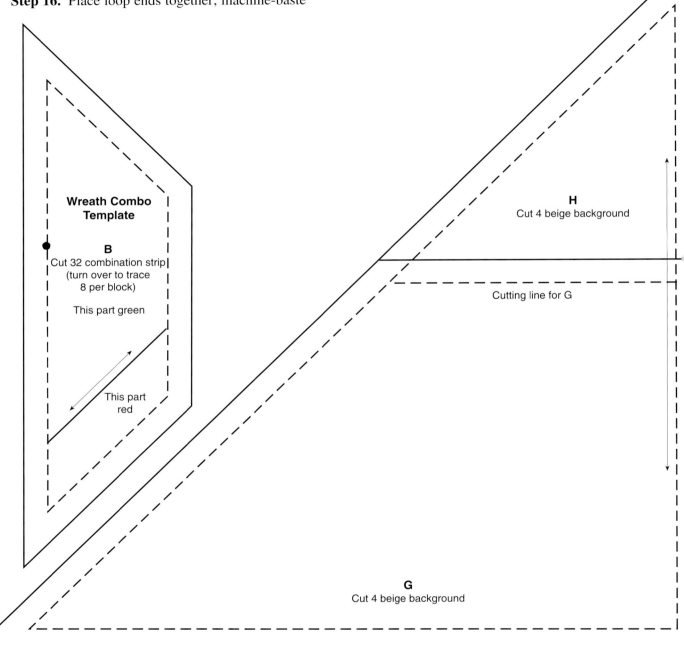

Wreath Combo Template

B
Cut 32 combination strip
(turn over to trace
8 per block)

This part green

This part red

H
Cut 4 beige background

Cutting line for G

G
Cut 4 beige background

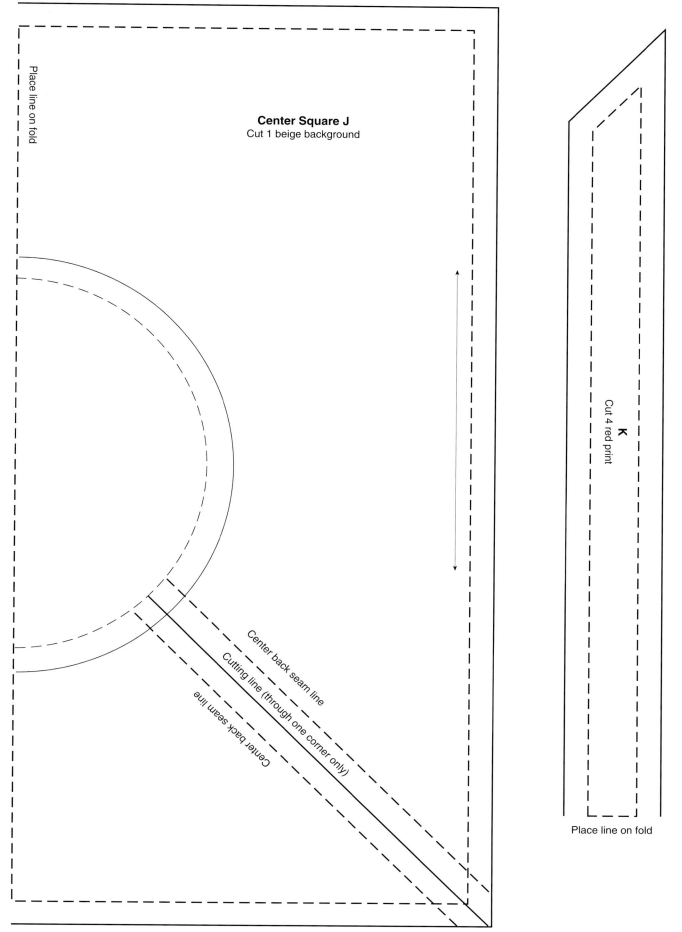

Center Square J
Cut 1 beige background

Place line on fold

Center back seam line
Cutting line (through one corner only)
Center back seam line

K
Cut 4 red print

Place line on fold

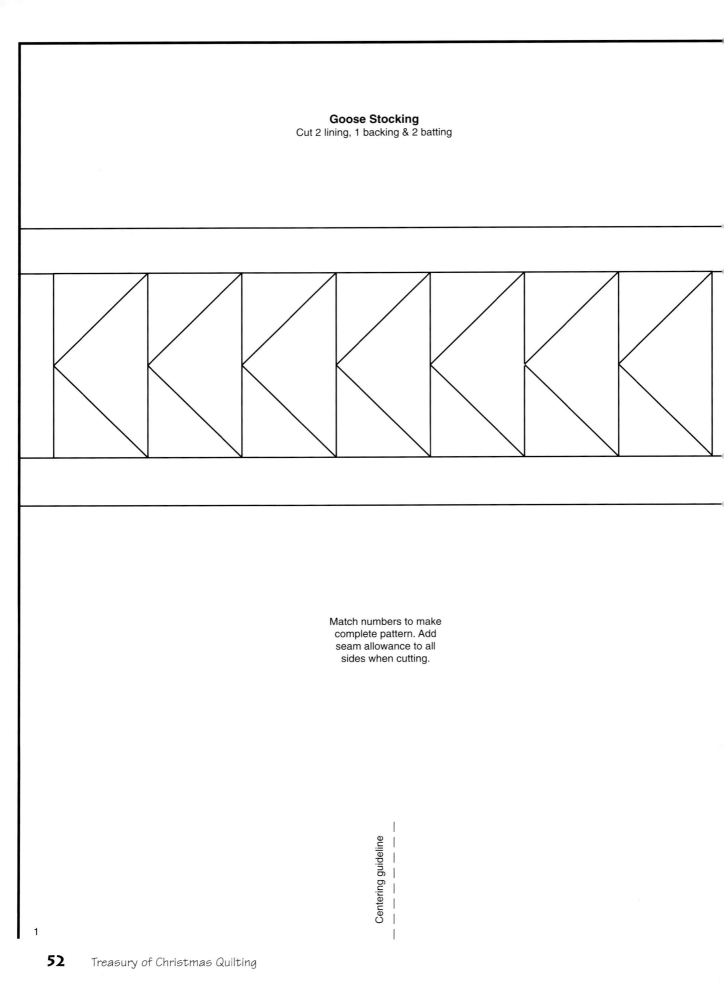

Goose Stocking
Cut 2 lining, 1 backing & 2 batting

Match numbers to make
complete pattern. Add
seam allowance to all
sides when cutting.

Centering guideline

1

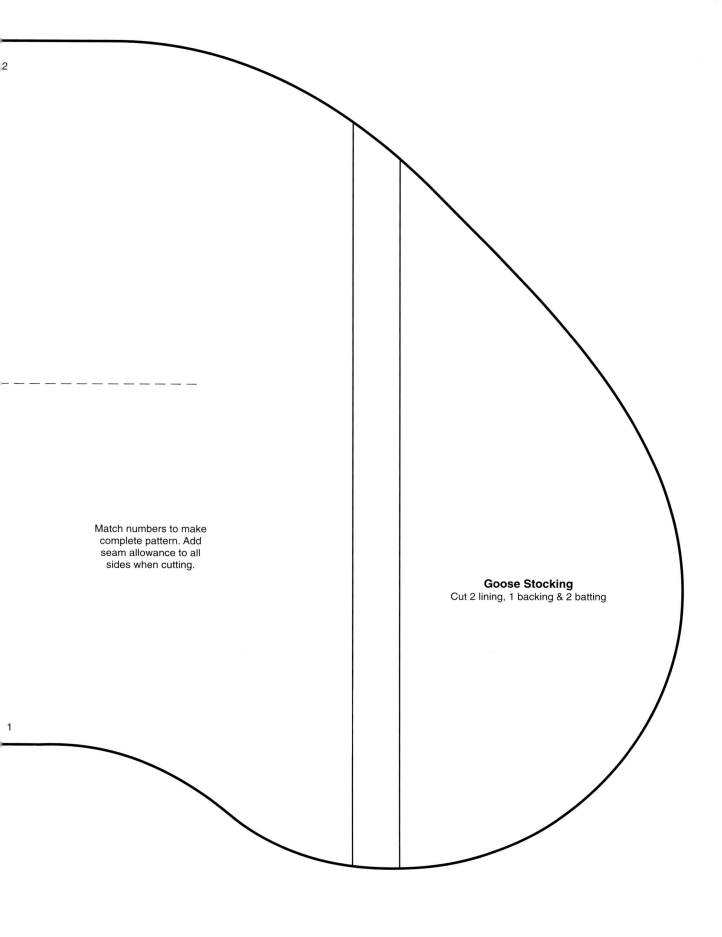

2

Match numbers to make
complete pattern. Add
seam allowance to all
sides when cutting.

Goose Stocking
Cut 2 lining, 1 backing & 2 batting

1

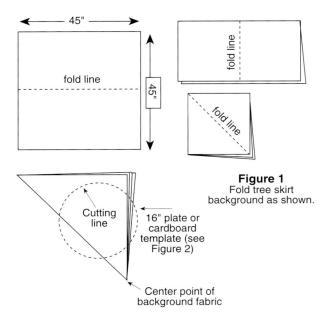

THEY PROCLAIM HIS GLORY

By Elizabeth Kuennen

So many times when Christmas comes along we get caught up in the holiday rush. In all the hustle and bustle, we tend to forget the true meaning of Christmas for Christians—the birth of Jesus Christ.

We read in Luke 2:8–14 that the angels announced Jesus' birth to shepherds in the fields, saying (Verse 14): "Glory to God in the highest, and on Earth peace among men with whom He is pleased" (New American Standard Version). Also in Matthew 2:1–2 and verses 9 and 10 we hear of the magi, or wise men, who were guided to the Christ child by a star.

Project Specifications

Skill Level: Easy
Ornament Size: 4 1/4" x 4 1/4"
Wall Hanging Size: 18" x 20"
Tree Skirt Size: Approximately 42" diameter

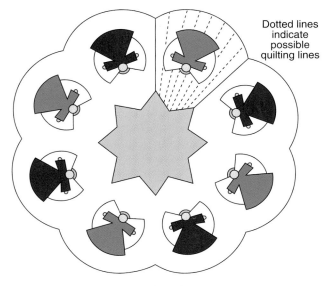

Angel Tree Skirt
Placement Diagram
Approximately 42" Diameter

TREE SKIRT

Materials

- 1 1/4 yards background fabric
- 1/2 yard gold lamé for star and halos
- 1/4 yard each of 2 different fabrics for angel dresses
- 1/3 yard fabric for wings
- Scraps peach fabric for head and hands
- 2 yards fusible transfer web
- Batting 46" x 46"
- Backing 46" x 46"
- 5 1/2 yards self-made or purchased binding
- 4 1/2 yards ruffled lace or eyelet (optional)
- All-purpose threads to match fabrics
- 1 spool quilting thread
- Thin typing paper
- Freezer paper
- 16" round object or pencil, 8" string and large piece of cardboard
- Thin-line permanent marker

Instructions

Note: Printed muslin was used for the background fabric in the project shown. Lamé was used for the angels' faces. Because the angels were fused and then machine-appliquéd to the background, the lamé did not require fusible interfacing. We recommend that all cotton fabrics be washed and ironed before using; do not wash the lamé.

45"

45"

fold line

fold line

fold line

fold line

Figure 1
Fold tree skirt background as shown.

Cutting line

16" plate or cardboard template (see Figure 2)

Center point of background fabric

ORIGAMI CHRISTMAS ORNAMENTS

By Nancy Brennan Daniel

Origami is the traditional Japanese paper-folding technique. Use fabric instead of paper to create these marvelous ornaments.

Use no-sew methods to create unique fabric ornaments. If you prefer to stitch the ornaments rather than glue them, it takes just a little more time, but not enough to notice.

Project Specifications
Skill Level: Easy
Ornament Sizes: 4" and 5"

Materials
For Each Ornament
- 2 squares fabric either 7" or 9"
- 1 piece fusible transfer web the same size
- 6" piece ribbon
- Fabric glue
- Optional: small purchased Christmas trim

Instructions
Step 1. Fuse the fabric squares together with the fusible transfer web following manufacturer's instructions.

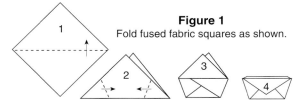

Figure 1
Fold fused fabric squares as shown.

Step 2. Fold the square as shown in Figure 1.

Step 3. Stitch or glue the flaps closed.

Step 4. Fasten a little Christmas trim to each side of the ornament.

Step 5. Stitch or glue a 6" ribbon along each side for a handle/hanger.

SO-EASY CHRISTMAS ORNAMENTS

By Elizabeth Kuennen

What do you do when you need a Christmas gift and you have only about an hour to make one? Make these so-easy ornaments!

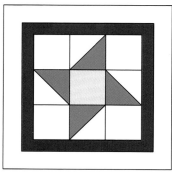

Star or Windmill
3 1/2" x 3 1/2" Block

Ohio Star
3 1/2" x 3 1/2" Block

Cactus Basket
3 1/2" x 3 1/2" Block

Whether you choose to use these designs for ornaments or package decorations, or even change the colors and give them as Mother's Day or Easter presents, you will have fun making them.

Project Specifications
Skill Level: Easy
Ornament Size: 3 1/2" x 3 1/2"

Materials
For 4 Ornaments
- 1/8 yard backing fabric (muslin or white fabric recommended) or 1 piece light-colored heavyweight construction paper, oak tag or watercolor paper 8 1/2" x 11"
- Scraps of Christmas prints at least 3 1/4" square
- 1/8 yard paper-backed fusible transfer web
- Fine-tipped permanent black, gold or silver marker
- Small amount of fiberfill or leftover batting

Instructions
Step 1. Trace the chosen pattern directly onto the paper side of the fusible webbing by placing the webbing directly over the pattern and tracing it using a sharp lead pencil. *Note: To make it easier to trace the patterns, either cut the patterns given out of the book or photocopy them and tape them to a table or hard surface using masking tape. Place the transfer webbing over the patterns; tape in place to prevent the webbing from shifting while you trace; remove tape when finished. Cut out individual pieces.*

Step 2. Iron the fusible webbing piece to the wrong side of the chosen fabric scrap following the instructions given by the manufacturer.

Step 3. Carefully cut along pattern lines. *Note: Accuracy is important; if the pattern is not cut precisely, there will be gaps between the pieces after they are ironed onto the backing.*

Step 4. Cut the outside border pieces. *Note: The border is a one-piece frame. It could be made using four shorter strips with mitered or butted corners if you don't have large scraps.*

Step 5. Apply fusible transfer webbing to border pieces.

Step 6. Repeat above steps for all pieces of each ornament.

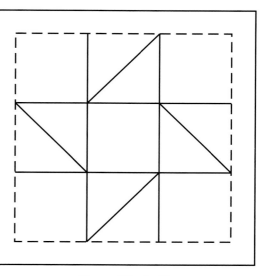

Star or Windmill
2 3/4" x 2 3/4" Block

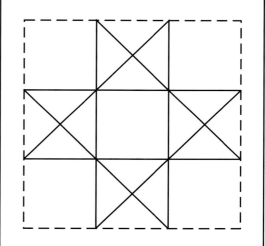

Ohio Star
2 3/4" x 2 3/4" Block

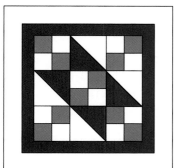

Jacob's Ladder
3 1/2" x 3 1/2" Block

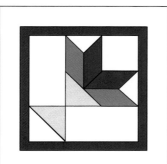

Basket
3 1/2" x 3 1/2" Block

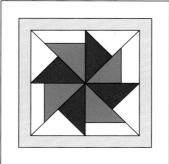

Pinwheel
3 1/2" x 3 1/2" Block

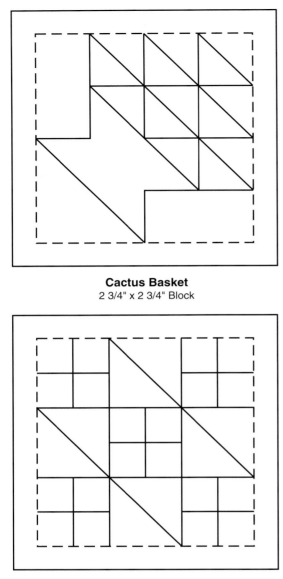

Cactus Basket
2 3/4" x 2 3/4" Block

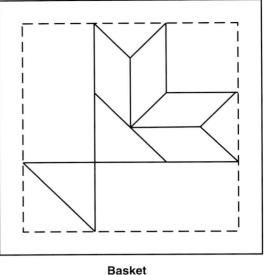

Basket
2 3/4" x 2 3/4" Block

Jacob's Ladder
2 3/4" x 2 3/4" Block

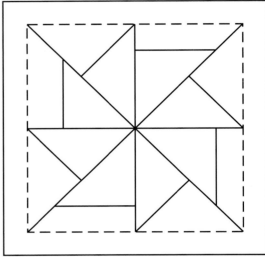

Pinwheel
2 3/4" x 2 3/4" Block

Step 7. Cut four squares 4" x 4" from backing fabric or paper.

Step 8. Remove paper backing from pattern pieces by gently rolling up the edge of the pieces to loosen the paper.

Step 9. Place the border piece or pieces on the backing fabric right side up or on paper backing first, then iron as directed by the webbing manufacturer. ***Note: When using paper or oak tag as a backing material, use a dry iron or the paper will warp.***

Step 10. Place the remaining pattern pieces on the backing in their correct positions inside the border; iron in place.

Step 11. Square up the fabric-backed pieces to 4" x 4", if necessary; trim the paper-backed pieces to 3 1/2" x 3 1/2" square, centering the design. ***Note: A rotary cutter may be used, but remember to use a dull blade for cutting paper; save the good blades for fabric.***

Step 12. Draw a dashed line with a fine-tipped permanent marker close to the edges of the pieces to simulate quilting lines.

Step 13. For pillow-type ornaments, cut one piece of fabric 4" x 4" for each ornament.

Step 14. Place this piece right sides together with prepared fused top; sew around outside leaving a 1 1/2"–2" opening. Trim corners, turn right side out and stuff; slipstitch the opening closed.

Step 15. Add an 8" piece of string, thread or narrow ribbon to each ornament for hanging. For paper ornaments, glue the thread to the back with tacky glue or a low-melt glue gun; or punch a small hole in the top and run the thread through the hole. For the pillow-type ornaments, thread a needle with the string, thread or narrow ribbon and pull it through the material on the top edge; remove the thread from the needle and tie to finish.

CHRISTMAS IN THE COUNTRY

By Beth Wheeler

Homey fabrics in stripes, checks, flowers and plaids add country charm to our tree skirt and matching stocking.

Project Specifications
Skill Level: Intermediate
Tree Skirt Size: 45" diameter
Stocking Size: 13 1/4" x 14 3/4"

TREE SKIRT

Materials
- 8 (1/4-yard) pieces cotton fabrics in red, tan, green and black
- 1/2-yard pieces of 2 fabrics for patchwork
- 1 1/2 yards muslin
- 2 yards of 2 contrasting fabrics for ruffle
- Supplies and tools: rotary cutter, self-healing mat and ruler, rotary wave blade or pinking shears,

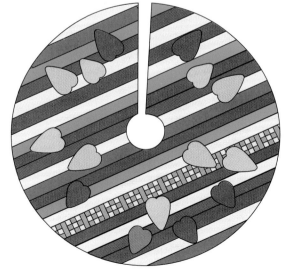

Country Tree Skirt
Placement Diagram
45" Diameter

tracing paper, pencil and scissors
- Fairfield Processing's Soft Touch cotton quilt batt
- 1 spool all-purpose neutral color thread
- 1 spool fine monofilament

- 1 skein black embroidery floss
- Several flat buttons
- HeatnBond Lite fusible sheet
- Fade-out marker or chalk pencil
- Crochet thread

Project Notes

Stitch with a 1/4" seam allowance unless otherwise noted.

During stitch-and-flip steps, make sure strip will cover batting edge when flipped open.

Avoid fabrics that ravel easily. If such fabric is chosen for ruffling, cut strips on the bias to avoid excess raveling.

Instructions

Step 1. Cut a 45" circle (or largest circle possible) from muslin and batting with scissors as shown in Figure 1. Cut center and opening.

Figure 1
Fold fabric and cut as shown
to make a circle.

Step 2. Layer the muslin and batting; pin layers together. Machine-baste to hold.

Step 3. Mark an angle on batting side with ruler and fade-out pen or chalk pencil as shown in Figure 2.

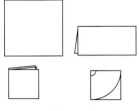

Figure 2
Mark an angle on the circle as shown.

Step 4. Cut three 1 1/2" by fabric width strips of the two fabrics for patchwork with straight blade in rotary cutter. Cut one 1 1/4", two 1 1/2", two 1 3/4" and one 2" strip of each red, tan, black and green fabric from selvage to selvage with straight blade in rotary cutter.

Step 5. Stitch one strip each of patchwork fabrics A and B together along one long edge; press seams open. Stitch another strip fabric A along B as shown in Figure 3; press seams open.

Step 6. Stitch one strip each fabrics B and A together along one long edge; press seams open. Stitch another strip fabric B along A as shown in Figure 4; press seams open.

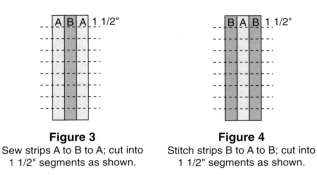

Figure 3
Sew strips A to B to A; cut into
1 1/2" segments as shown.

Figure 4
Stitch strips B to A to B; cut into
1 1/2" segments as shown.

Step 7. Cut 1 1/2" slices from each strip set. Stack one slice of each trio together, right sides facing, as shown in Figure 5; repeat for 18 stacks. Stitch; press seams open.

Step 8. Stitch remaining slices on each unit for a total of nine blocks as in Figure 6 and nine blocks as shown in Figure 7. Press seams open.

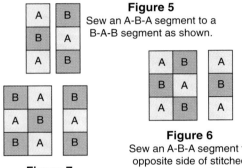

Figure 5
Sew an A-B-A segment to a
B-A-B segment as shown.

Figure 6
Sew an A-B-A segment to
opposite side of stitched
segments as shown.
Complete 9 blocks.

Figure 7
Sew a B-A-B segment to
opposite sides of stitched
segments as shown.
Complete 9 blocks.

Step 9. Join alternating blocks with a 1 1/2" x 3 1/2" strip of any fabric between blocks as shown in Figure 8.

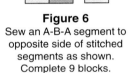

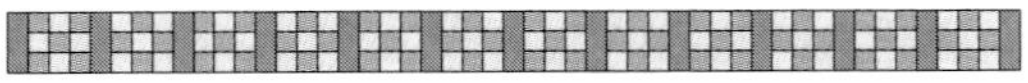

Figure 8
Join pieced units with strips as shown.

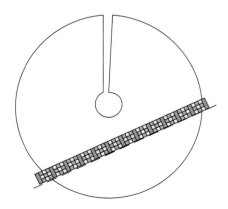

Figure 9
Place patchwork strip along
chalk line on batting.

Stitching

Step 1. Place patchwork strip along chalk line on batting, right side up. Pin in place with strip ends covering batting edge as shown in Figure 9.

Step 2. Place a second strip on top of the first, right sides together, as shown in Figure 10, making sure ends will cover batting edges when flipped open. Stitch along the right edge with 12–14 stitches per inch, using neutral thread. Finger-press open as shown in Figure 11.

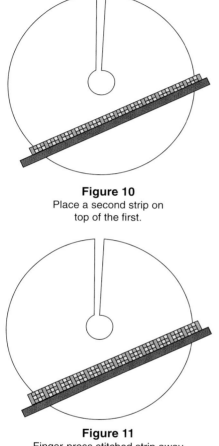

Figure 10
Place a second strip on
top of the first.

Figure 11
Finger-press stitched strip away
from patchwork strip as shown.

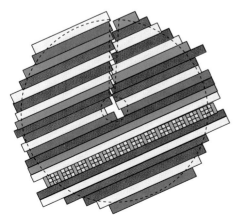

Figure 12
Continue adding strips of
varying widths until batting
piece is covered.

Step 3. Repeat procedure, placing strips of varying widths, colors and values next to one another. Continue stitching and finger-pressing open until entire batting piece is covered as shown in Figure 12.

Step 4. Press with steam iron. Stitch all around tree skirt 1/2" away from edge; trim to 3/8" with wave blade in rotary cutter. Leave raw pinked edges for a folk-art look, or bind with bias binding for a finished look.

Finishing

Step 1. Cut 14 strips 1 1/4" wide of one ruffle fabric along the length of the fabric with wave blade in rotary cutter. This fabric will be on top. Cut 14 strips of remaining ruffle fabric 1 3/4" wide along length of fabric with wave blade. This fabric will be on bottom.

Step 2. Lay a piece of crochet thread down the center of each strip. Zigzag over crochet thread by machine with monofilament thread in top and neutral thread in bobbin. Pull crochet thread gently to gather strips for ruffle as you sew. ***Note:*** *The zigzag stitch should clear crochet thread on both sides—this makes removal easier later.* When you reach the end of one fabric strip, overlap the next strip and continue stitching. Repeat with all ruffling strips.

Step 3. Placing wider ruffle on bottom and narrow ruffle on top, pin ruffle around outside of tree skirt, matching centers of ruffle with stitching on skirt. Zigzag through skirt and both ruffles with monofilament in machine top and neutral thread in bobbin.

Step 4. Remove crochet thread.

Embellishment

Step 1. Place tracing paper over heart patterns. Trace with pencil; cut out with scissors.

Step 2. Bond fusible sheet to wrong side of fabric scraps; remove paper backing.

Step 3. Fuse scraps of batting between two fabric scraps.

Step 4. Place tracing paper on fused fabric; trace with fade-out pen or chalk pencil. Trace 16 assorted hearts; cut out with wave blade in rotary cutter. Stitch 1/4" from edge. Set one heart aside for stocking.

Step 5. Arrange randomly on tree skirt.

Step 6. Stitch hearts on tree skirt with black embroidery floss threaded through a button, as in photograph.

STOCKING

Materials

- Scrap strips cotton fabrics in red, tan, green and black from tree skirt
- Scrap of patchwork from tree skirt
- 1/4 yard muslin
- Scraps of ruffle from tree skirt
- 1/2 yard backing fabric

- 1 stitched heart from tree skirt
- Thread: neutral sewing and fine monofilament
- Black embroidery floss
- Flat button
- Lightweight fusible transfer web
- Fade-out marker or chalk pencil
- Crochet thread
- Supplies and tools: rotary cutter, self-healing mat and ruler, rotary wave blade or pinking shears, sewing machine, tracing paper, pencil, scissors and usual sewing supplies

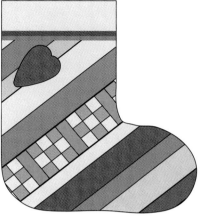

Country Stocking
Placement Diagram
13 1/4" x 14 3/4"

Instructions

Step 1. Place tracing paper over stocking patterns. Trace with pencil; cut out. Prepare full-size stocking pattern referring to Figure 13.

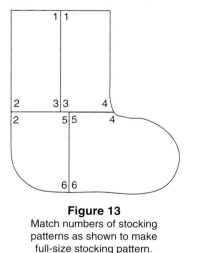

Figure 13
Match numbers of stocking patterns as shown to make full-size stocking pattern.

Step 2. Cut two muslin, one batting and one backing from stocking pattern. Layer one muslin and one batting stocking; pin. Mark an angled line on batting side with ruler and fade-out pen or chalk pencil.

Step 3. Place patchwork scrap along line. Position another strip on patchwork, right sides

together. Stitch; finger-press open; pin.

Step 4. Repeat stitch-and-flip process until entire stocking is covered. Press; trim with scissors.

Step 5. Place pieced stocking panel and stocking back piece together, right sides facing; place muslin lining on top. Stitch with a 1/2" seam allowance; clip curves. Turn and press.

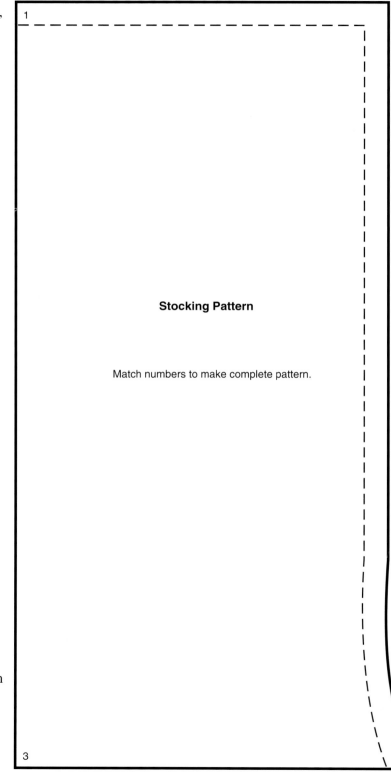

Stocking Pattern

Match numbers to make complete pattern.

Step 6. Cut a 9" x 15" piece backing fabric for cuff; hem along short ends with 1/2" seam allowance. Press seam open; fold in half with wrong sides together.

Step 7. Apply double ruffle scraps along seam and around folded edge with monofilament threaded in the top of the machine. Stitch; remove crochet thread.

Step 8. Stitch cuff along top raw edge of stocking with rights sides of cuff facing lining side of stocking; fold stitched cuff piece up and over stocking top to cover seam. ***Note:*** *All but about 1/2" of the stitched cuff piece will be folded over to the right side.*

Step 9. Cut two 1" x 7" pieces patterned fabric with wave blade for hanging loop. Stitch 1/4" away from each edge. Fold in half; stitch along seam.

Step 10. Stitch one heart on front of stocking with black embroidery floss threaded through one button.

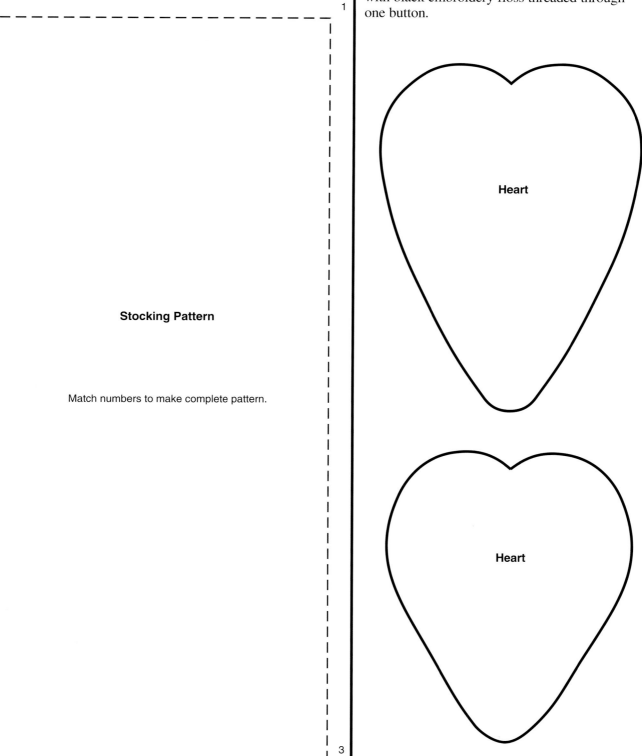

1

Stocking Pattern

Match numbers to make complete pattern.

2

3

Heart

Heart

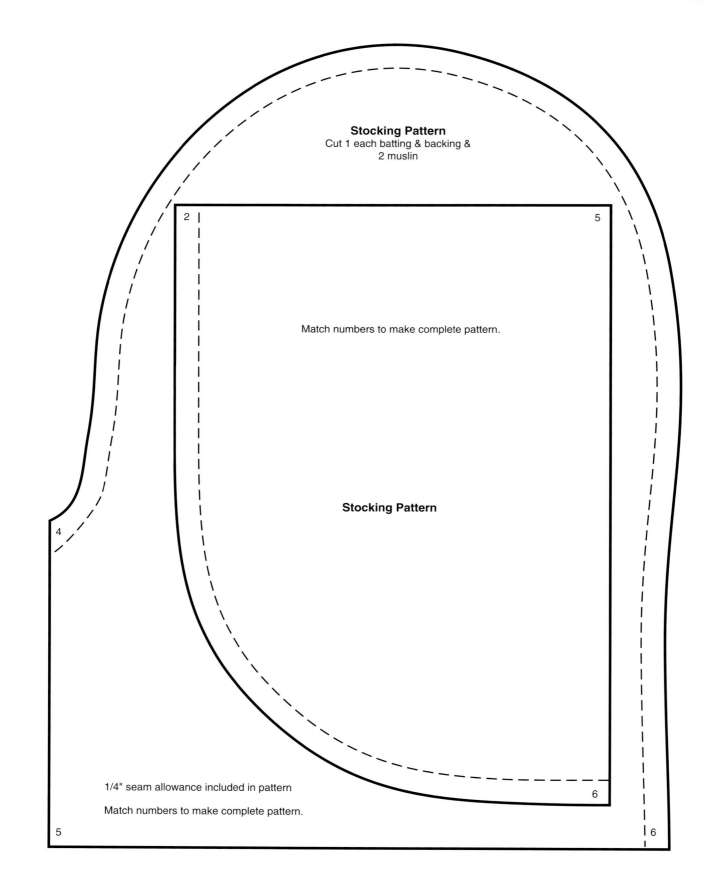

Stocking Pattern
Cut 1 each batting & backing &
2 muslin

2   5

Match numbers to make complete pattern.

Stocking Pattern

4

1/4" seam allowance included in pattern

Match numbers to make complete pattern.

6

5   6

SUE ANGEL

By Beth Wheeler

It's the night before Christmas and Sue Angel is busy replacing lost stars in the sky. She takes her job very seriously, for only the most faithful angels are blessed with this special job!

Project Specifications
Skill Level: Intermediate
Wall Hanging Size: 20" x 30"
Stocking Size: 12" x 15"

WALL HANGING

Materials
- 2 woven (not terry) 100 percent cotton tea towels (approximately 20" x 30")
- Scraps cotton fabrics in red, white, blue, green, solid peach and yellow
- Lightweight fusible sheet
- Tracing paper and pencil
- Soft Touch cotton quilt batting 24" x 34"
- 1 spool very fine monofilament thread
- 1 spool each red, peach and white all-purpose threads
- Navy blue embroidery floss or pearl cotton

- Assorted buttons or beads
- Cord for hanging (optional)
- 6 tea bags

Sue Angel Wall Hanging
Placement Diagram
20" x 30"

Project Note

All fabrics in the sample were tea-dyed by simmering in 4 cups of water with six tea bags for 20 minutes, allowed to air-dry then pressed with a steam iron to remove wrinkles.

Instructions

Step 1. To make rod pocket for hanging, cut one strip scrap fabric 3" by length of towel. Press 1/2" hem on each short end; machine-stitch with coordinating thread in upper machine and bobbin. Press 3/8" under along each long edge; set aside.

Step 2. Bond fusible sheet to wrong side of fabric scraps following manufacturer's directions.

Step 3. Place tracing paper over patterns. Trace with pencil; cut out with scissors.

Step 4. Place pattern pieces on paper side of fused scraps. Trace with pencil; cut out; remove paper backing.

Step 5. Arrange pieces on one towel, referring to the Placement Diagram and photo. Fuse in place, following manufacturer's directions.

Step 6. With coordinating thread in machine top and white thread in machine bobbin, stitch around angel pieces with a medium-width satin stitch.

Step 7. Work buttonhole stitch (Figure 1) around each remaining shape with hand-sewing needle and 3 strands embroidery floss or one strand pearl cotton.

Figure 1
Make buttonhole stitch as shown.

Finishing

Step 1. Layer towels with slightly smaller piece of batting between; pin in place.

Step 2. Stitch along detail lines of angel, stars and trees by hand or machine using monofilament thread to add dimension.

Step 3. Echo-quilt around motifs, as in Figure 2.

Step 4. Buttonhole-stitch around periphery of towel with hand-sewing needle and 3 strands embroidery floss.

Step 5. Add buttons with embroidery floss to decorate trees and embellish stars.

Step 6. Position rod pocket along edge of top back. Pin along both long edges. Hand-stitch long edges with hand-sewing needle and coordinating thread to finish.

Figure 2
Echo-quilt around shapes.

STOCKING

Materials

- Woven 100 percent cotton tea towel (approximately 20" x 30")
- Scraps cotton fabrics in blue, red, green and yellow
- 1/2 yard muslin (for lining)
- Lightweight fusible sheet
- Tracing paper and pencil
- Feather Touch cotton quilt batting
- 1 spool very fine monofilament thread
- Navy blue embroidery floss or pearl cotton
- Assorted buttons or beads

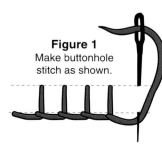

Sue Angel Stocking
Placement Diagram
12" x 15"

Instructions

Step 1. Place tracing paper over stocking patterns given on pages 66–68. Trace tree and star patterns; cut out.

Step 2. Bond fusible sheet to wrong side of fabric scraps, following manufacturer's directions.

Step 3. Place stocking pattern on towel with hemmed edge along stocking top. Trace two stocking pieces on towel, reversing one. Trace two stocking pieces on muslin and one on batting; cut out.

Step 4. Place tree and star patterns on paper side of fused scraps. Trace with pencil; cut out and remove paper backing.

Step 5. Arrange motifs on one towel piece referring to the Placement Diagram and photo. Fuse in place, following manufacturer's directions.

Step 6. Work buttonhole stitch around each shape with hand-sewing needle and 3 strands of embroidery floss. Decorate trees and embellish stars with buttons and 3 strands of navy embroidery floss.

Step 7. Layer embellished towel stocking and batting piece; pin in place.

Quilting

Step 1. Stitch along detail lines of stars and trees by hand or machine with monofilament to add dimension.

Step 2. Echo-quilt around motifs.

Step 3. Place front and back together, right sides facing. Stitch with a 1/2" seam allowance.

Step 4. Trim seam allowances, clip curves; turn right side out.

Step 5. Place muslin pieces together; stitch with a 1/2" seam allowance. Trim seam allowances; clip curves. Press 3/8" around top toward wrong side. Slip lining inside stocking. Slip-stitch together around stocking top with hand-sewing needle and thread.

Step 6. Work a buttonhole stitch around stocking top with hand-sewing needle and 3 strands navy embroidery floss to finish.

Trees
Cut as many green scraps as desired

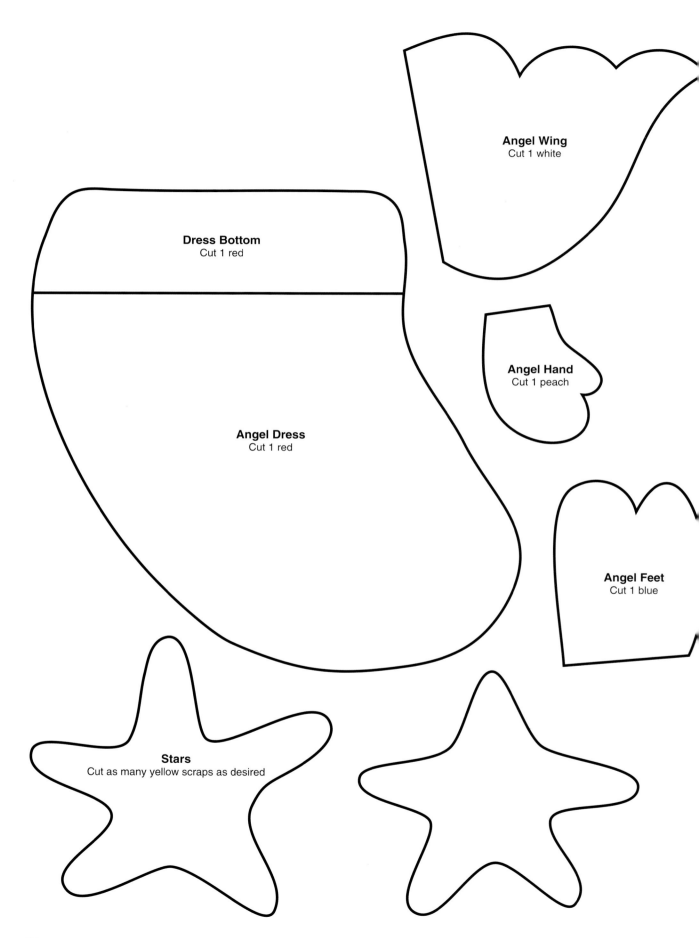

Angel Wing
Cut 1 white

Dress Bottom
Cut 1 red

Angel Hand
Cut 1 peach

Angel Dress
Cut 1 red

Angel Feet
Cut 1 blue

Stars
Cut as many yellow scraps as desired

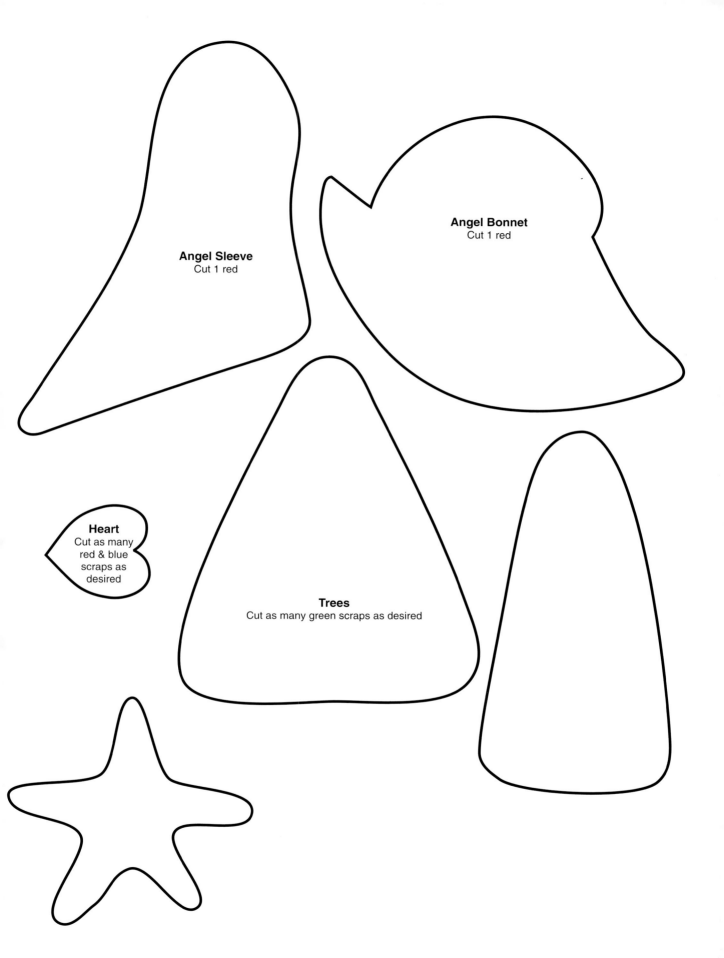

Angel Sleeve
Cut 1 red

Angel Bonnet
Cut 1 red

Heart
Cut as many
red & blue
scraps as
desired

Trees
Cut as many green scraps as desired

HOLLY GARLAND

By Judi Kauffman

Hang this garland in a doorway, over your
mantel or any location where it would drape
nicely. Make it longer and use it on your tree!

Have fun creating this easy fabric garland using
small Log Cabin blocks connected with red yo-
yos. Make it as long as you need, adding more blocks
and yo-yos to lengthen.

Holly Garland
Placement Diagram
Approximately 5" x 32"

Project Specifications

Skill Level: Easy
Block Size: 4" x 4"
Garland Dimensions:
Approximately 5" x 32"

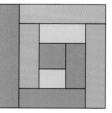

Log Cabin
4" x 4"

Materials

- 12 (3 1/4") circles red print
- 5 squares 1 1/2" x 1 1/2"
  bright green
- Assorted 1 1/4"-wide strips
  green prints
- Red and green all-purpose thread
- 5 squares Pellon Thermolam Plus batting
  4 1/2" x 4 1/2"
- 5 backing squares 4 1/2" x 4 1/2"
- 2 pieces red/green stripe 3/8"-wide ribbon
  24" long

Instructions

Step 1. Turn under 1/4" on each circle; using red
thread, sew a stitch around the turned edges. Pull

stitches to gather as shown in Figure 1; knot to hold. Repeat for 12 yo-yos.

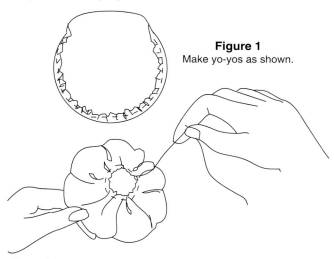

Figure 1
Make yo-yos as shown.

Step 2. Join three yo-yos together at edges using secure hand stitches as shown in Figure 2.

Figure 2
Join 3 yo-yos as shown.

Step 3. Starting with the 1 1/2" green squares, sew green strips to each side of the square in Log Cabin fashion until you have added two strips to each side of the center referring to Figure 3 for order of piecing. Trim strips even with stitched section after adding each strip. Press and square up to 4 1/2" x 4 1/2"; repeat for five blocks.

Figure 3
Piece Log Cabin block as shown.

Step 4. Layer one square of batting, backing and pieced square (right sides facing); sew around edges leaving part of one side open for turning. Trim corners and turn right side out; blind-stitch the opening closed.

Step 5. Join the blocks together with the yo-yos between with secure stitches to make one long garland.

Step 6. Fold ribbon pieces in half; sew one to each end to form a tie for hanging.

TAPESTRY DELIGHTS

By Beth Wheeler

What can you do with those sample cuts of tapestry and drapery fabric scraps from the reupholstering project? The fabric is much too expensive to waste even one square inch! Try our decidedly distinguished bear or sophisticated stocking to use up some odd-shape scraps.

Project Specifications
Skill Level: Experienced
Bear Size: 18" tall
Stocking Size: 12" x 15"

TEDDY BEAR
Materials
- Scraps or sample cuts of tapestry fabrics in burgundy, cream and teal
- Scrap burgundy velveteen
- Tracing paper and chalk pencil
- Seam sealant
- 12 ounces polyester fiberfill
- Wooden spoon
- 1 spool sturdy neutral thread
- 1 spool monofilament thread
- Awl or other pointy tool
- 4 (35mm) sets doll joints
- Assorted scraps lace and trims
- Assorted buttons, beads and charms
- Ribbon roses
- 3/4 yard ribbon or cord

Project Notes
Making teddy bears is not easy. Using specialty fabrics instead of fur doesn't allow for the mistakes that fur can hide.

The fun thing about making bears is that every one you make has a personality all its own. Embellish your bears with a variety of trims and laces and have fun assembling a whole family of related bears.

Instructions
Note: All pattern pieces include a 1/4" seam allowance.

Step 1. Place tracing paper over patterns; trace and cut out.

Step 2. Cut paw pads and foot pads from velveteen. Cut body parts from assorted tapestry fabrics. Apply thin line of seam sealant to all cut edges to prevent raveling.

Step 3. Stitch laces and trims on body parts (Figure 1) by machine fitted with monofilament thread in top and a neutral thread in bobbin.

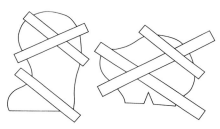

Figure 1
Arrange lace pieces on tapestry body parts in crazy-quilt fashion as shown.

Step 4. Place two ear pieces right sides together; repeat. Stitch around ears with a 1/4" seam allowance, using a neutral thread in top and bobbin, leaving an opening as indicated on pattern. Clip curves; turn right side out. Close opening with hand-sewing needle and thread.

Step 5. Stitch darts in head sides. Stitch sides together from nose to neck (A–X). Stitch head gusset to head sides from nose to back of neck (A–B).

Step 6. Clip curves; apply seam sealant to any edges that may ravel easily. Turn head right side out.

Step 7. Stitch paws to inner arms; press seams open. Place inner arm and outer arm together, right sides facing; stitch, leaving opening for turning. Clip curves; apply seam sealant; turn right side out.

Step 8. Place leg pieces together, right sides facing; stitch, leaving opening for turning. Stitch foot pad in place. Clip all curves; apply seam sealant. Turn legs right side out.

Body

Step 1. Pin body center fronts together, right sides facing. Stitch; press seam open. Stitch backs together, leaving opening as indicated on pattern. Stitch front to back; do not turn.

Step 2. Slip turned head inside body; match center fronts and center backs. Stitch head to body; turn right side out through center back opening.

Step 3. Stuff head firmly with fiberfill; packing with wooden spoon.

Step 4. Make holes for arm joints in bear body and one arm with awl as indicated on pattern. Insert male half of joint through hole in arm from inside. Push point of male half through hole in bear body; slip washer over point of male half; snap anchor in place to secure joint. Repeat for remaining arm.

Step 5. Repeat with legs and remaining joints.

Step 6. Stuff arms firmly with fiberfill, packing tightly with wooden spoon. Close opening with hand-sewing needle and neutral thread.

Step 7. Stuff legs firmly with fiberfill; pack tightly; close opening.

Step 8. Stuff body firmly with fiberfill; pack tightly; close opening. Fold pleat in ears; pin in place. Secure with hand-sewing needle and thread.

Step 9. Stitch assorted buttons, ribbon roses, ribbons, charms and beads on bear to embellish. Tie ribbon or cord in a bow around bear's neck.

STOCKING

Materials

- Scraps or sample cuts of tapestry fabrics in burgundy, cream and teal
- 1/4 yard muslin (for lining)
- Scrap burgundy velveteen
- Tracing paper and chalk pencil
- Seam sealant
- Cotton batting 15" x 19"
- Neutral color sewing thread
- Assorted scraps lace, ribbons and trims
- Assorted buttons
- Coordinating or contrasting cord
- 2 tassels

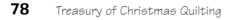

Tapestry Stocking
Placement Diagram
12" x 15"

Instructions

Step 1. Place tracing paper over stocking pattern on pages 66–68. Trace and cut out.

Step 2. Trace two stocking pieces on muslin with chalk pencil; cut out. Trace two stocking pieces on batting 1" larger all around pattern; cut out.

Step 3. Lay one scrap of tapestry fabric on batting as shown in Figure 2. Position a lace or trim scrap on top; stitch in place along long edges. Place another fabric scrap on top of first, right sides facing; stitch along one edge; flip open. Place another lace or trim scrap on fabric; stitch in place along long edges. Repeat until stocking piece is covered in crazy-quilt fashion.

Joint

Leg
Cut 4 tapestry scraps
(reverse half)

Leave open for turning

Step 4. Place embellished stocking piece on ironing board, batting side up. Cover with press cloth; press with steam iron (dry iron if using velvet, velveteen or other fabric with nap).

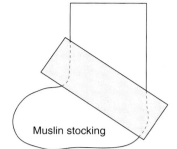

Muslin stocking

Figure 2
Lay tapestry pieces on muslin
stocking as shown.

Step 5. Place paper pattern on embellished stocking piece; cut to size.

Step 6. Place embellished stocking piece right sides together with a large

tapestry scrap; cut out using embellished stocking as a pattern; stitch around stocking pieces with 1/2" seam allowance, leaving top open. Clip curves; turn right side out.

Step 7. Place muslin lining pieces together, right sides facing. Stitch around stocking lining with 1/2" seam allowance; clip curves.

B

X

Center back

Place line on fold

Head Gusset
Cut 1 tapestry scrap

A

X

A

Dart

Head Side
Cut 2 tapestry scraps
(reverse 1)

Ear placement

B

Step 8. Place lining inside stocking, matching front and back seams; baste through all layers around stocking top.

Finishing

Step 1. Cut 11" x 16" strip from velveteen for cuff; fold in half crosswise. Stitch along short ends with a 1/4" seam allowance. Press seam allowance open; turn right side out.

Step 2. Fold cuff in half lengthwise; press.

Step 3. Place cuff inside stocking, matching cuff seam with back stocking seam. Stitch around top through all layers with a 1/4" seam allowance.

Step 4. Fold cuff up; press seam allowance. Fold cuff to right side of stocking, encasing raw edges.

Step 5. Stitch cord around stocking periphery by hand using coordinating thread, forming a loop for hanging at the top.

Step 6. Add buttons, ribbons and beads randomly with hand-sewing needle and thread.

Step 7. Stitch tassels on cuff, referring to photo for ideas.

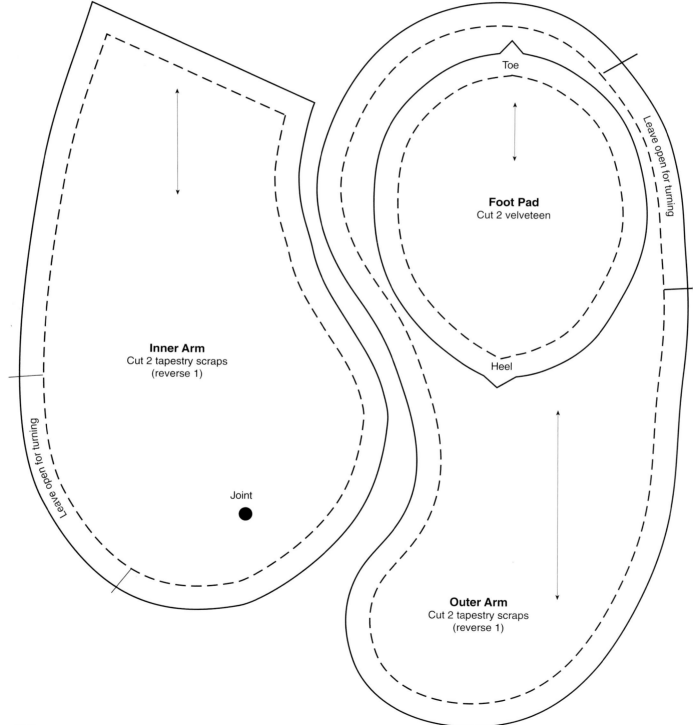

Foot Pad
Cut 2 velveteen

Toe

Heel

Leave open for turning

Inner Arm
Cut 2 tapestry scraps
(reverse 1)

Leave open for turning

Joint

Outer Arm
Cut 2 tapestry scraps
(reverse 1)

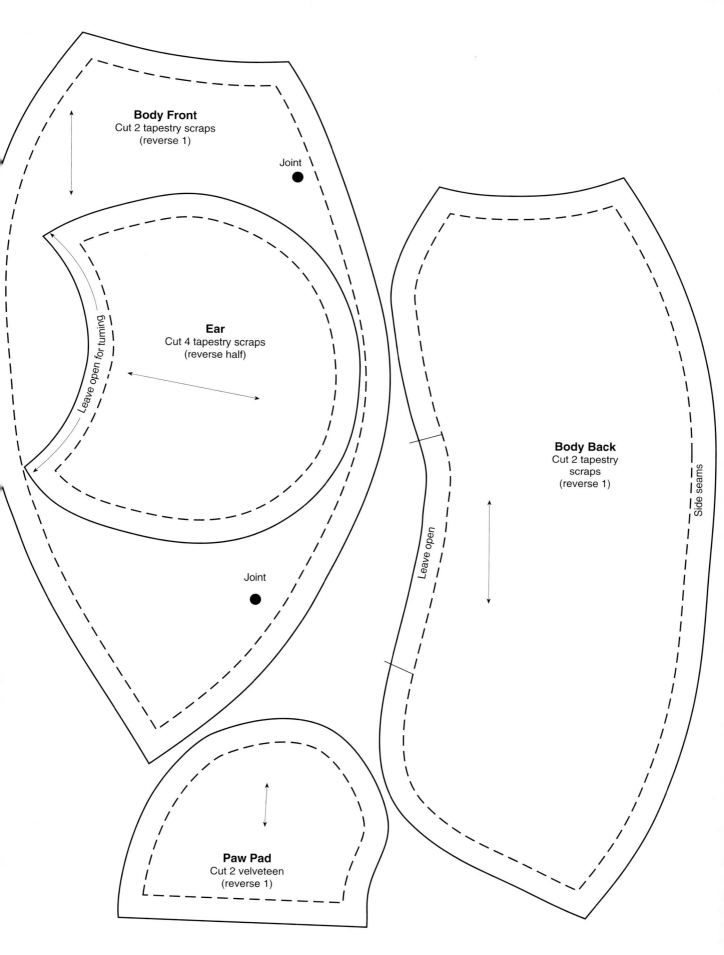

Body Front
Cut 2 tapestry scraps
(reverse 1)

Joint

Ear
Cut 4 tapestry scraps
(reverse half)

Leave open for turning

Joint

Body Back
Cut 2 tapestry
scraps
(reverse 1)

Leave open

Side seams

Paw Pad
Cut 2 velveteen
(reverse 1)

ISOBEL ANGEL TREE TOPPER

By Beth Wheeler

Isobel tries to be a good little angel. She sits on the treetop and attempts to look perfect. Yes, the other angels know her stocking has a hole in the toe, her halo is askew and she's always late for choir practice. But the love in her heart makes Isobel a joy to those around her. Won't you invite Isobel to grace your treetop and spread her warm love to your household?

Project Specifications
Skill Level: Intermediate
Angel Size: Approximately 7 1/2" x 12"

Materials
- Large scrap muslin
- Scraps of pink plaid, print and solid
- Scrap white fabric
- Scrap peach solid
- Lightweight fusible sheet
- Fabric glue
- Tracing paper and chalk pencil
- Feather Touch cotton quilt batting
- 1 spool monofilament thread
- 1 spool each peach, pink and white all-purpose threads
- Navy blue embroidery floss
- 9 ribbon rosebuds
- Star garland or trim (for halo)
- Scrap pink felt
- 30 yards narrow garment-grade ribbon (not craft ribbon)

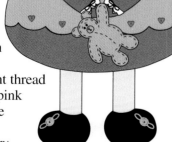

**Isobel Angel
Tree Topper**
Placement Diagram
Approximately 7 1/2" x 12"

- Curling rods or several small-diameter metal knitting needles or wooden kitchen skewers
- Cotton swab
- Fine-tip black or brown permanent marker
- Black acrylic paint
- Paintbrush
- Cosmetic blusher
- 4 tea bags

Project Notes
The size of ribbon curls is determined by the size of the curling rod and the ribbon. Small-diameter rods or knitting needles and very narrow ribbon will produce the tightest curls.

Feather Touch cotton batting is needle-punched, making it possible to stitch directly to the batting. Stitching directly on any other brand batting may cause tearing and shredding.

Instructions
Step 1. Tie a knot in one end of ribbon; slip into slot on end of curling rod or onto point of knitting needle. Wind ribbon along length of rod in a spiral so rounds do not overlap. Wrap ribbon through slot twice or tie to other end of knitting needle. Repeat with entire length of ribbon.

Step 2. Dampen ribbon with clear water. Place rods on baking sheet in warm (200-degree) oven for at least one hour.

Step 3. Remove from oven; cool completely before touching. When cool, release ends and push ribbon off rods.

Step 4. Tea-dye large scrap of peach fabric in two cups of water with four tea bags for 15 minutes. Squeeze liquid from fabric; press dry with iron.

Step 5. Place tracing paper over patterns. Trace and cut out.

Step 6. Place teddy bear pattern on felt. Trace two bears; cut out.

Step 7. Add details with fine-tip permanent marker. Glue two bears together. Press between two heavy books to dry flat.

Step 8. Bond fusible sheet to wrong side of large scrap peach fabric and scraps pink print, pink plaid, pink solid and white fabric following manufacturer's directions.

Angel Front

Step 1. Place body pattern on muslin; trace around it with chalk pencil—do not cut out.

Step 2. Place pinafore pattern on paper side of pink print; trace pinafore. Fit dress hem pattern into scallops at bottom of pinafore pattern; trace. Pin print and plaid fabrics together; cut scallop edge through both fabrics at the same time to ensure a perfect fit later. Finish cutting pinafore and dress hem.

Step 3. Trace and cut one face from peach fabric. Trace and cut two collars (one reversed) from white fabric.

Step 4. Remove paper backing from all five pieces. Position on muslin body inside chalk outline; fuse in place, following manufacturer's directions.

Step 5. Trace seven hearts on paper side of solid pink fabric; cut out. Place one heart in each scallop on dress; set remaining two hearts aside. Fuse hearts in place along pinafore hem.

Step 6. Satin-stitch along scalloped hem and dress periphery with pink thread, around collars with white and all around face with peach. Add facial features with fine-tip marker referring to Figure 1. Apply cosmetic blusher in cheek area with cotton swab.

Figure 1
Add facial features to face piece.

Step 7. Stitch around hearts with monofilament thread in machine top using a blind-hem or narrow zigzag stitch.

Construction

Step 1. Fuse two scraps of peach together. Place leg pattern on fused peach; trace two legs; cut out.

Step 2. Apply black paint on shoe area; let dry; apply second coat, if necessary.

Step 3. Place legs on backside of body front referring to the Placement Diagram. Stitch across legs just below dress hem.

Step 4. Cut 3/8" away from chalk lines for seam allowance. Cut one piece each of muslin and batting to match. Layer body front with batting; pin through all layers. Quilt along detail lines with monofilament in sewing machine.

Step 5. Straight-stitch along collar and scalloped hem with hand-sewing needle and 3 strands embroidery floss.

Step 6. Cut one body piece each from muslin, pink print and batting, adding 3/8" seam allowance. Layer print body back with batting body; pin in place. Quilt as desired for angel's back.

Step 7. Place body front and back together, right sides facing. Stitch from dot around body; stop at dot on other side. Trim curves; clip seam allowances. Turn shell right side out; press.

Step 8. Place muslin lining pieces together, stitch from dot to dot. Trim; clip, but do not turn.

Step 9. Press shell and lining hem seam allowances to wrong side. Slip lining inside shell; stitch lining to shell along head seam with hand-sewing needle and thread. Slipstitch lining to shell along hemline.

Finishing

Step 1. Cut two wings from plaid fabric and one from batting, adding a 3/8" seam allowance. Place fabric wings together, right sides facing; place batting wings on top. Stitch along seam line, leaving open as indicated on pattern.

Step 2. Clip curves; trim corners. Turn right side out. Close opening with hand-sewing needle and coordinating thread. Press well with pressing cloth and steam iron.

Step 3. Straight-stitch around periphery of wings with hand-sewing needle and 3 strands navy embroidery floss.

Step 4. Fuse remaining pink hearts on wings, referring to the photo. Stitch around hearts with monofilament thread using a blind-hem or zigzag stitch.

Step 5. Stitch wings to back of angel where pieces overlap with hand-sewing needle and thread.

Step 6. Cut four sleeves from plaid; stitch two sets right sides together, leaving an opening for turning. Clip curves; turn right side out. Stuff lightly with fiberfill. Close opening with hand-sewing needle and thread. Stitch eyelet around sleeve bottom for cuff with hand-sewing needle and thread. Tie two bows from 6-strand embroidery floss; stitch one on each cuff.

Step 7. Stitch sleeves on shoulders with hand-sewing needle and thread, referring to the Placement Diagram.

Embellishing

Step 1. Stitch one ribbon rose in the center of each fused heart and one on each shoe toe.

Step 2. Stitch teddy bear to Isobel's hands. Tie bow from 6-strand embroidery floss. Stitch bow under Isobel's chin.

Step 3. Cut several short snippets of curled ribbon for bangs. Stitch or glue in place on forehead.

Step 4. Cut curled ribbon into 8" lengths. Gather lengths in a bundle 3" x 8". Tie a bow with 6 strands embroidery floss 2" from each end as shown in Figure 2.

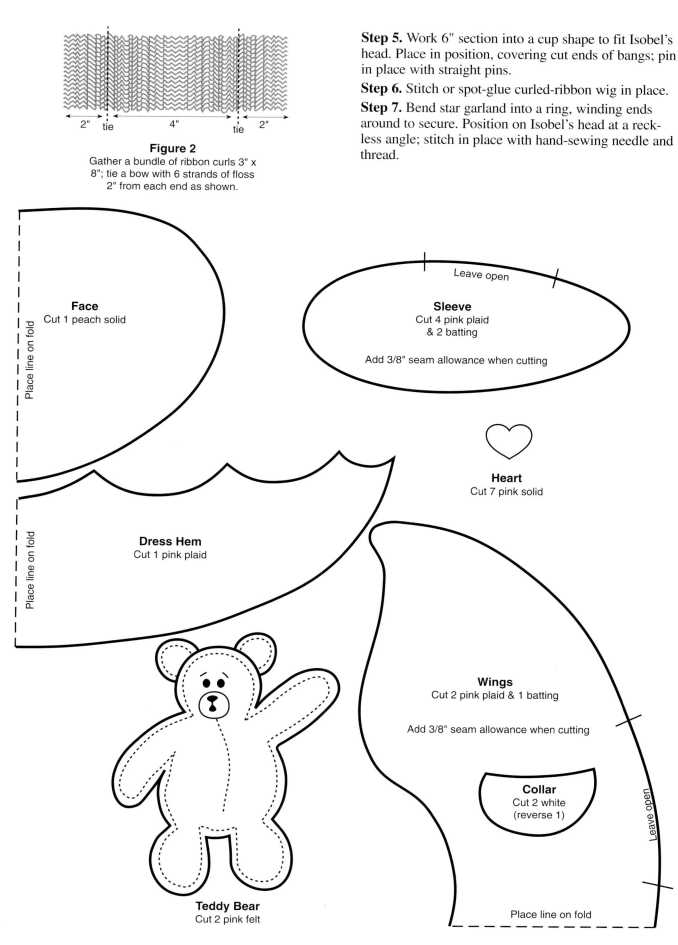

Figure 2
Gather a bundle of ribbon curls 3" x
8"; tie a bow with 6 strands of floss
2" from each end as shown.

2" tie 4" tie 2"

Step 5. Work 6" section into a cup shape to fit Isobel's head. Place in position, covering cut ends of bangs; pin in place with straight pins.

Step 6. Stitch or spot-glue curled-ribbon wig in place.

Step 7. Bend star garland into a ring, winding ends around to secure. Position on Isobel's head at a reckless angle; stitch in place with hand-sewing needle and thread.

Place line on fold

Face
Cut 1 peach solid

Leave open

Sleeve
Cut 4 pink plaid
& 2 batting

Add 3/8" seam allowance when cutting

Heart
Cut 7 pink solid

Place line on fold

Dress Hem
Cut 1 pink plaid

Wings
Cut 2 pink plaid & 1 batting

Add 3/8" seam allowance when cutting

Collar
Cut 2 white
(reverse 1)

Leave open

Teddy Bear
Cut 2 pink felt

Place line on fold

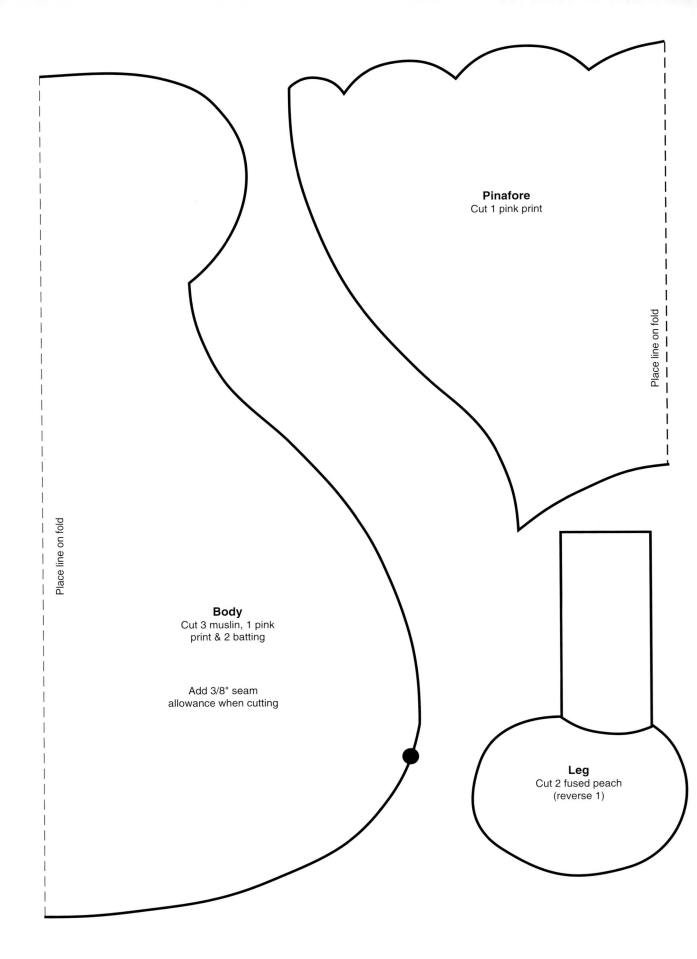

Pinafore
Cut 1 pink print

Place line on fold

Place line on fold

Body
Cut 3 muslin, 1 pink
print & 2 batting

Add 3/8" seam
allowance when cutting

Leg
Cut 2 fused peach
(reverse 1)

CHRISTMAS TREE SKIRT

By Lucy A. Fazely

This spiderweb-design tree skirt is quick and easy to make using strips of Christmas prints.

When you can stitch a project without using any templates, it saves so much time. This easy tree skirt is one of those projects. Make up a couple of these at a time. Keep one for yourself and give the others away.

Project Specifications
Skill Level: Easy
Tree Skirt Size: 43" in diameter

Materials
- 1/4 yard each light, light-to-medium, medium and medium-to-dark Christmas prints
- 3/4 yard dark Christmas print (includes binding)
- Backing 45" x 45"
- Batting 45" x 45"
- 45-45-90-degree ruler
- 24" quilter's ruler

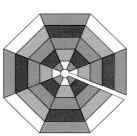

Placement Diagram
43" Diameter

Instructions
Note: A 1/4" seam allowance is included in all measurements.

Step 1. Cut two strips from each fabric 4 1/2" by fabric width.

Step 2. Sew one strip of each fabric together starting with the lightest fabric and working toward the darkest fabric as shown in Figure 1. Repeat for a second set; press seam allowances toward the darkest fabric.

Figure 1
Sew fabric strips together from light to dark.

Step 3. Lay the 45-degree-angle ruler on one pieced fabric strip as shown in Figure 2. *Note: If your ruler has parallel lines marked on it, these lines will be parallel with the seams on the fabric strip.* Lay the long

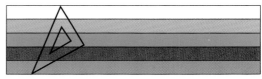

Figure 2
Place 45-degree ruler on strips with lines on ruler parallel to seams on strip.

ruler next to the angled ruler as shown in Figure 3. Shift the rulers as far to the edge of the fabric as you can without getting off the fabric to ensure you have enough of the pieced strip from which to cut your wedges.

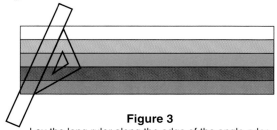

Figure 3
Lay the long ruler along the edge of the angle ruler.

Step 4. Making sure the 45-degree ruler is in the right position and that the straight ruler is butted up against it, remove the 45-degree ruler and cut the fabric along the edge of the long ruler.

Step 5. Position the 45-degree ruler so the point is right up to and even with the shorter side of the pieced strip and running even with the edge of the fabric as shown in Figure 4. Place the long ruler along side the 45-degree ruler; move the 45-degree ruler and cut along the line made by the long ruler as shown in Figure 5.

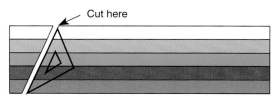

Figure 4
Cut along the edge of the long ruler to make the angle.

Figure 5
Repeat for other side of angle ruler; cut along edge of long ruler.

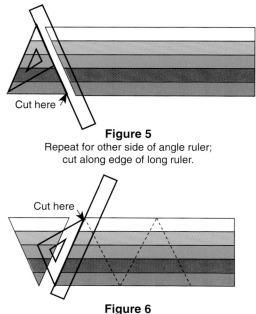

Figure 6
Place ruler on the bottom of the strip with ruler along the side; repeat cutting.

Step 6. Continue to cut a total of four wedge-shaped pieces from each strip as shown in Figure 6. You should have four pieces that are dark on the long end and four that are light on the long end. Handle the pieces carefully so as not to stretch the bias edges.

Step 7. To make room for the tree trunk, trim the sharp points on each of the pieces as shown in Figure 7. For an artificial tree, trim 1 1/2" from each point. For live trees, trim 2 1/2" from each point.

Step 8. Arrange wedge pieces as shown in Figure 8. Sew the wedges together except for one seam for the side opening. Press all seam allowances in the same direction.

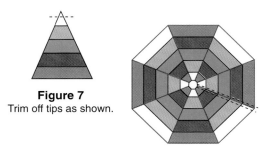

Figure 7
Trim off tips as shown.

Figure 8
Join wedges as shown. Trim 1/4" seam allowance off the 2 wedges at the opening.

Step 9. Trim the seam allowance off on the sides that will remain open as shown in Figure 8; baste the edges to keep the bias-cut fabric from stretching out of shape.

Step 10. Sandwich batting between prepared backing pieces and completed top, keeping the raw basted edges right next to each other but not overlapping; baste layers together.

Step 11. Quilt in the ditch of all seams or as desired by machine.

Step 12. Trim off excess batting and backing. Cut through batting and backing along opening to center of quilt. Remove excess backing and batting from quilt center.

Step 13. Use remaining 1/2 yard of dark fabric to make self-made bias binding. Trim all edges to form an even rectangle. Place the 90-degree angle ruler in one corner as shown in Figure 9; trim off corner. Cut remaining piece into 2 1/2"-wide strips as shown in Figure 10.

Figure 9
Trim a rectangle as shown.

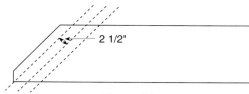

Figure 10
Continue cutting 2 1/2"-wide strips at the same angle.

Step 14. Sew bias strips with right sides together on short ends to make one continuous strip as shown in Figure 11; press seams open. Press strip in half with wrong sides together.

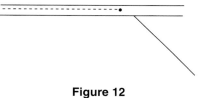

Figure 11
Join the angled strips on the short ends.

Step 15. Leaving a 6"–8" tail of binding, start sewing binding to any straight edge of the tree skirt with a 3/8" seam, matching all raw edges. On inside and outside corners, stop at seams and pivot binding. On the four corners, at the opening of the tree skirt, miter the binding by sewing to within 3/8" from the corner as shown in Figure 12. Without cutting the thread, remove the quilt a few inches from under the sewing machine needle.

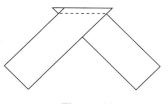

Figure 12
Sew strip to within 3/8" from corner.

Step 16. Fold the binding up so it is perpendicular to the last stitches as shown in Figure 13. Fold the bind-

ing down so it is parallel to the side of the tree skirt to be bound next. Resume sewing from the edge of the quilt as shown in Figure 14.

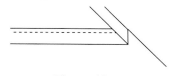

Figure 13
Fold strip up and away as shown.

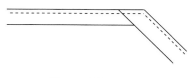

Figure 14
Fold back down and stitch.

Step 17. To finish, stop sewing binding about 8" from where you started. Lay the binding flat along quilt edge; fold back onto itself where the two ends meet as shown in Figure 15. Press these folds to crease. Open binding and sew right sides together using crease as a stitching line. Trim seam allowance to 1/4" press open and re-fold bias lengthwise. Finish sewing binding to tree skirt edge.

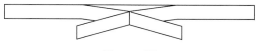

Figure 15
Join the ends at crease as shown.

Step 18. Turn binding to back of quilt; stitch in place using a blind stitch to finish.

CHRISTMAS STAR BANNER

By Wendy Kinzler

Show the world how pretty Christmas fabrics look when used to make star designs! This pretty banner combines five different star patterns in an unusual setting.

Project Specifications

Skill Level: Advanced
Wall Hanging Size: Approximately 16" x 33"
Star Block Sizes: 4 1/4" x 4 1/4" and 12" x 12"

Materials

- 1 yard red print for borders
- 3/4 yard green print for background
- 1 yard white print
- Scraps red, green and white prints with seasonal motifs
- 1 strip muslin 4" by fabric width
- Batting 20" x 37"
- Backing 20" x 37"
- All-purpose threads to match fabrics
- 3 red tassels (optional)
- Bells or buttons (optional)
- 3 yards self-made or purchased binding

Christmas Stars
Placement Diagram
Approximately 16" x 33"

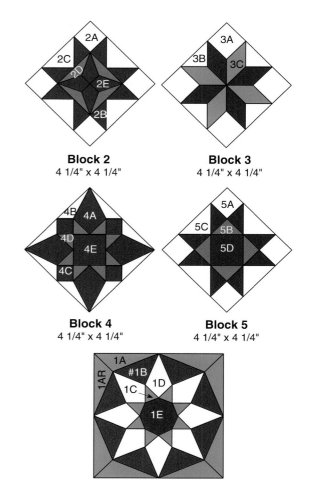

Block 2
4 1/4" x 4 1/4"

Block 3
4 1/4" x 4 1/4"

Block 4
4 1/4" x 4 1/4"

Block 5
4 1/4" x 4 1/4"

Block 1—Christmas Star
12" x 12"

Instructions

Step 1. Prepare templates using pattern pieces given. Label each piece and separate for individual patterns.

Step 2. Cut the fabric pieces for the center, Block 1, Christmas Star, using pieces #1A through #1E as directed on templates. To piece the block, set eight #1C's onto #1E. Set in eight #1D's, then #1B's. Add #1A and #1AR pieces to each corner to complete the block as shown in Figure 1; press and square up to 12 1/2" x 12 1/2" if necessary.

Step 3. Cut the fabric pieces for Block 2 using pieces #2A through #2E as directed on pattern pieces. To piece one block, sew four #2E pieces together, sewing only to the end of the marked seam line; set in four #2D's referring to Figure 2. Sew two #2B's to the two short sides of #2C; repeat three times. Add two #2A's to the ends of two of these units. Set the two short units onto two opposite sides of the center square. Add on the two remaining long strips to complete Block 2; press and square up to 4 3/4" x 4 3/4" if necessary.

Step 4. Cut the fabric pieces for Block 3 using pieces #3A through #3C as directed on pattern pieces. To piece one block, join eight #3C pieces to make star. Set in the #3A and #3B pieces to complete Block 3 referring to Figure 3; press and square up to 4 3/4" x 4 3/4" if necessary.

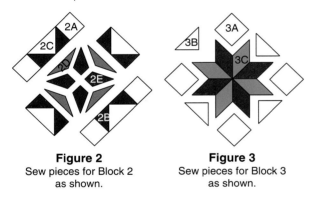

Figure 1
Sew pieces for Christmas Star block as shown.

Figure 2
Sew pieces for Block 2
as shown.

Figure 3
Sew pieces for Block 3
as shown.

Step 5. Cut the fabric pieces for Block 4 using pieces #4A through #4E as directed on pattern pieces. To piece one block, sew two #4D pieces to #4A; repeat for four units. Sew a unit to each side of #4E. Sew #4B and #4BR to #4C; repeat for four units. Set a unit in on each side of the previously pieced unit to complete Block 4 referring to Figure 4; press and square up to 4 3/4" x 4 3/4" if necessary.

Step 6. Cut the fabric pieces for Block 5 using pieces #5A through #5D as directed on pattern pieces. To

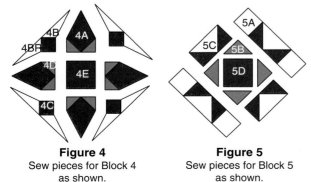

Figure 4
Sew pieces for Block 4
as shown.

Figure 5
Sew pieces for Block 5
as shown.

piece one block, sew a #5B piece to each side of #5D. Sew a #5B piece to each short side of #5C; repeat for four units. Sew one of these units to opposite sides of the previously pieced unit referring to Figure 5. Sew #5A to each end of the remaining two units; sew onto remaining sides to complete Block 5; press and square up to 4 3/4" x 4 3/4" if necessary.

Step 7. Cut three pieces muslin 1" x 12 1/2" for piece D. Sew a piece to the top and bottom of Block 1; set remaining piece aside. Cut one green print C square 4 3/4" x 4 3/4". Cut A and B pieces as directed on pattern pieces.

Step 8. Sew A and B to Blocks 2 and 3 to make row 1 referring to Figure 6; press.

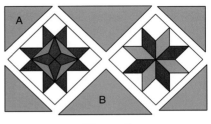

Figure 6
Join Blocks 2 and 3 with A and B
triangles as shown.

Step 9. Sew A, B and C pieces to Blocks 4 and 5 to make row 3 as shown in Figure 7; press.

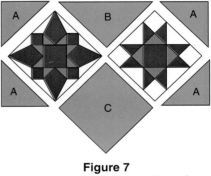

Figure 7
Join Blocks 4 and 5 with A, B and C
(4 3/4" x 4 3/4" square) as shown.

Step 10. Cut pieces E through H as directed on pattern pieces. Sew E, F, FR and ER to the bottom of row 3 as shown in Figure 8; press.

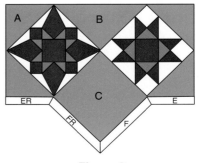

Figure 8
Sew E, ER, F and FR to the bottom of the A-B-C row.

Step 11. Join row 1 to row 2 to row 3 referring to Figure 9; press. Sew remaining D piece to the top of row 1; press.

Step 12. Cut two strips musin 1" x 26 1/2"; sew a strip to each long side of pieced center; press. Cut one strip red border print 2" x 13 1/2"; sew to top of pieced unit; press.

Step 13. Sew pieces G, H, GR and HR to the bottom of row 3; press.

Step 14. Cut two red print background strips 2" x 29 1/2"; sew a strip to each long side of pieced center; press.

Step 15. Mark the small quilting design given on the borders of the completed piece using a water-erasable marker or pencil.

Step 16. Sandwich batting between completed top and prepared backing piece. Pin or baste layers together to hold flat. Quilt on marked lines and as desired by hand or machine.

Step 17. When quilting is complete, remove pins or basting and trim edges even. Bind with self-made or purchased binding.

Step 18. Attach tassels at bottom corners and center point. Embellish with bells and buttons as desired.

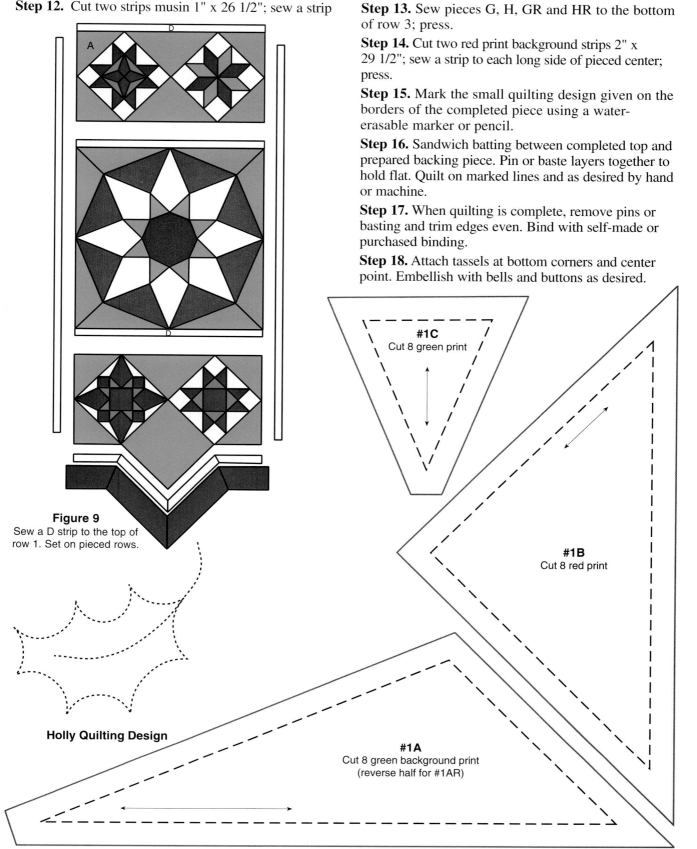

Figure 9
Sew a D strip to the top of row 1. Set on pieced rows.

Holly Quilting Design

#1C
Cut 8 green print

#1B
Cut 8 red print

#1A
Cut 8 green background print
(reverse half for #1AR)

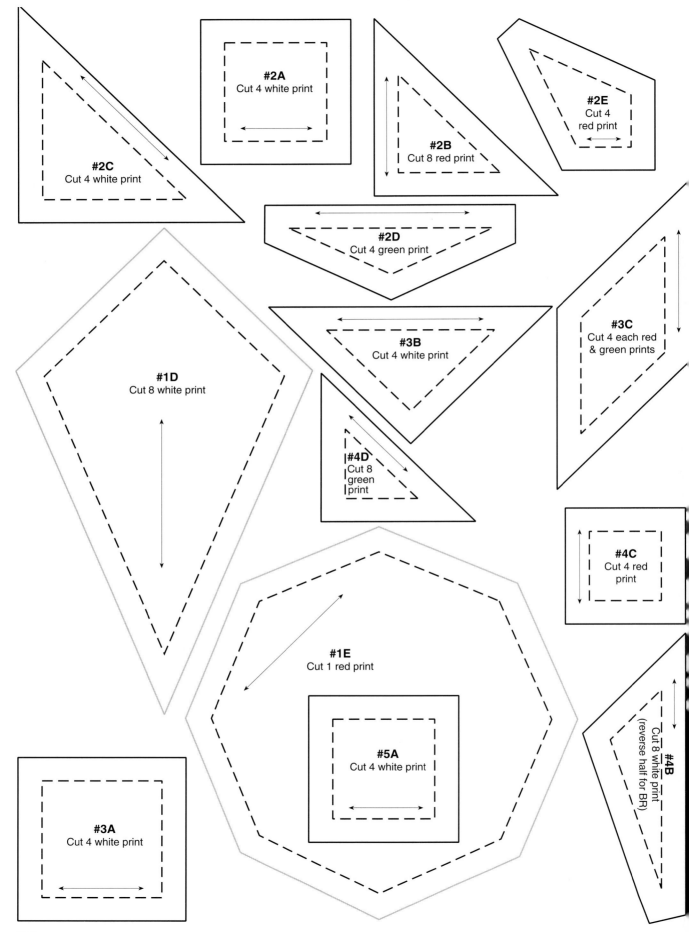

#2A
Cut 4 white print

#2C
Cut 4 white print

#2B
Cut 8 red print

#2E
Cut 4
red print

#2D
Cut 4 green print

#3B
Cut 4 white print

#3C
Cut 4 each red
& green prints

#1D
Cut 8 white print

#4D
Cut 8
green
print

#4C
Cut 4 red
print

#1E
Cut 1 red print

#5A
Cut 4 white print

#3A
Cut 4 white print

#4B
Cut 8 white print
(reverse half for BR)

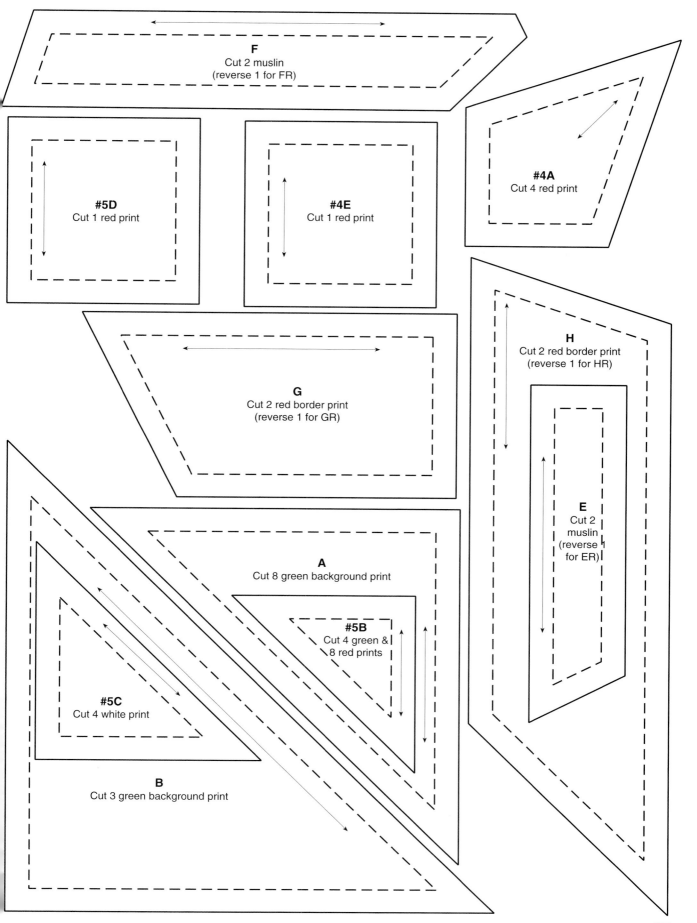

F
Cut 2 muslin
(reverse 1 for FR)

#4A
Cut 4 red print

#5D
Cut 1 red print

#4E
Cut 1 red print

H
Cut 2 red border print
(reverse 1 for HR)

G
Cut 2 red border print
(reverse 1 for GR)

E
Cut 2
muslin
(reverse 1
for ER)

A
Cut 8 green background print

#5B
Cut 4 green &
8 red prints

#5C
Cut 4 white print

B
Cut 3 green background print

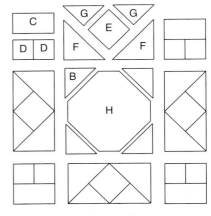

TIE A BOW AROUND A WREATH

By Doreen Burbank

This easy pieced wreath wall hanging features three-dimensional bows for a holiday bright spot on your wall or door.

Making pieced fabric pictures is fun—sort of like putting a puzzle together. Be careful placing the fabric pieces to create a pieced wreath design. Add tied fabric bows for a three-dimensional quality.

Project Specifications
Skill Level: Intermediate
Wall Hanging Size: 28" x 28"

Materials
- Scraps green print
- 1/2 yard red print for ribbons and bows
- 3/4 yard white background fabric
- Backing 30" x 30"
- Batting 30" x 30"
- 1 spool neutral color all-purpose thread
- 2 3/4 yards self-made or purchased binding

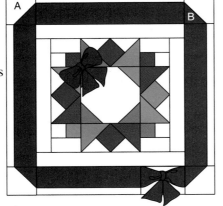

Christmas Wreath
Placement Diagram
28" x 28"

Instructions
Step 1. Prepare templates using pattern pieces given. Cut fabric patches as directed on each piece.

Step 2. Sew B to each corner of H. Sew G to two adjacent sides of E; add F to each remaining side. Repeat three times. Sew D to D; add C. Repeat three times. Set these units together as shown in Figure 1. Press completed pieced section.

Step 3. Cut two strips 2 1/2" x 16 1/2" white; sew to two opposite sides. Press seams toward strips. Cut two strips white 2 1/2" x 20 1/2"; sew a strip to the top and bottom. Press seams toward strips.

Figure 1
Sew pieces together as shown to piece 1 block.

Step 4. Cut three strips red 3 1/2" x 20 1/2" and three strips white 1 1/2" x 20 1/2". Sew a white strip to a red strip three times; press seams toward the red strip.

Step 5. Cut one white strip 1 1/2" x 14 1/2" and one red strip 3 1/2" x 14 1/2"; sew the white strip to the red strip. Cut a white strip 4 1/2" x 6 1/2". Sew this to the end of the 14 1/2" strip as shown in Figure 2. Stitch this strip unit to the bottom of the pieced center.

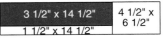

3 1/2" x 14 1/2"	4 1/2" x 6 1/2"
1 1/2" x 14 1/2"	

Figure 2
Sew the 4 1/2" x 6 1/2" white piece to the end of the 14 1/2" strip.

Step 6. Sew A to B four times; sew an A-B unit to each end of two of the red/white strip sections. Sew the remaining strip to the top of the pieced center; sew the A-B strips to the sides. Press seams toward the strips.

Step 7. To make bows, cut two pieces red 6 1/2" x 8 1/2". Fold each piece in half lengthwise right sides together; sew into an open-ended tube 3" x 8 1/2"; turn right side out and press.

Step 8. Cut two pieces red 3" x 3 1/2"; sew with right sides together along 3 1/2" sides to make small tubes. Turn right side out; press.

Step 9. Position the small tube around the center of the bow and pin in place temporarily. Sew ends of bows into seam lines referring to the photo and

CHRISTMAS QUILTS GREAT & SMALL

Whether you choose to make a bed-size quilt or a small wall hanging, Christmas quilts add warmth to your home during the holiday season. Use them as door decorations, on a coffee table, over the back of a chair or on a bed.

Quilts make wonderful long-lasting gifts which become heirlooms with the passing of time. Give a gift that will always be remembered for many years to come. Give a quilt this Christmas.

POINSETTIA QUILT

By Margaret C. Weatherby

More than 40 years ago I ordered a pattern through the mail. I kept it all this time, and when I finally decided to use it, I changed it to suit my taste. I hope you enjoy the design as much as I enjoyed using it .

Project Specifications
Skill Level: Intermediate
Block Size: 10" x 10" Block
Quilt Size: 89" x 109"

Materials
- 3 1/2 yards white with red dots
- 5 yards white solid
- 3 yards green solid
- 3 yards dark green small print
- 2 1/2 yards red solid for border strips
- Optional: 3 1/2 yards solid white for lining flowers
- 2 skeins each red, yellow and dark green embroidery floss
- Backing 93" x 113"
- Batting 93" x 113"
- 11 yards self-made or purchased binding

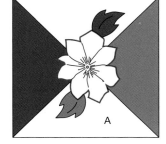

Poinsettia
10 x 10" Block

Project Note
The dark green background will show through the white poinsettia leaves. To eliminate this problem, line the B pieces with white by sewing a plain white B to a print B with right sides together. Leave an opening to turn the flower right side out.

This method finishes the edges of appliquéd pieces at the same time. It does give the flower a bulky layer to quilt through if quilting by hand. An alternate method would be to trim the dark green away from beneath the flowers when appliqué is complete.

Instructions
Step 1. Prepare templates using pattern pieces given.

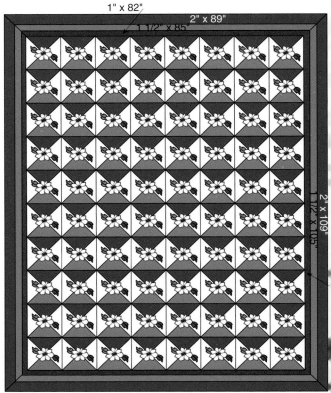

Poinsettia Quilt
Placement Diagram
89" x 109"

Cut as directed on each piece to complete the quilt as shown, adding a 1/4" seam allowance to appliqué pieces when cutting for hand appliqué.

Step 2. Sew a white A triangle to each green solid and dark green print A triangle; join referring to Figure 1, using all triangles.

Step 3. Turn under edges of appliqué pieces and baste to hold. *Note: If you choose to line the flowers, cut the same number of white solid flower pieces; sew with right sides together leaving an opening to turn. Turn*

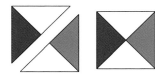

Figure 1
Sew white and green A triangles together and join to make a square as shown.

Figure 2
Center appliqué shapes on blocks as shown.

right side out, close opening and appliqué in place. Place the B flower on the block, centering at triangle intersection as shown in Figure 2; pin in place.

Step 4. Place the C leaves under the petals. Appliqué these in place first, then the B flower using either a hand-appliqué or buttonhole stitch. If using a buttonhole stitch, use 3 strands of red floss on B flowers and 3 strands of green floss on the leaves. Stitch the stamens using red floss with yellow French knots in the center.

Step 5. Cut two strips red solid 1 1/2" x 102 1/2" and two strips 1 1/2" x 82 1/2". Add shorter

strips to top and bottom and longer strips to sides, mitering corners; press.

Step 6. Cut two strips green solid 2" x 105 1/2" and two strips 2" x 85 1/2". Sew shorter strips to top and bottom and longer strips to sides, mitering corners; press.

Step 7. Cut two strips green print 2 1/2" x 109 1/2" and two strips 2 1/2" x 89 1/2". Sew shorter strips to top and bottom and longer strips to sides, mitering corners; press.

Step 8. Mark the quilt top for quilting using a water-erasable marker or pencil. The quilt shown was quilted in a cross-hatch design on the background and in the ditch around appliqué shapes.

Step 9. Sandwich batting between prepared backing piece and finished top. Baste layers together to hold flat. Quilt on marked lines and as desired.

Step 10. When quilting is complete, trim edges even and bind with self-made or purchased binding to finish.

Continued on page 158

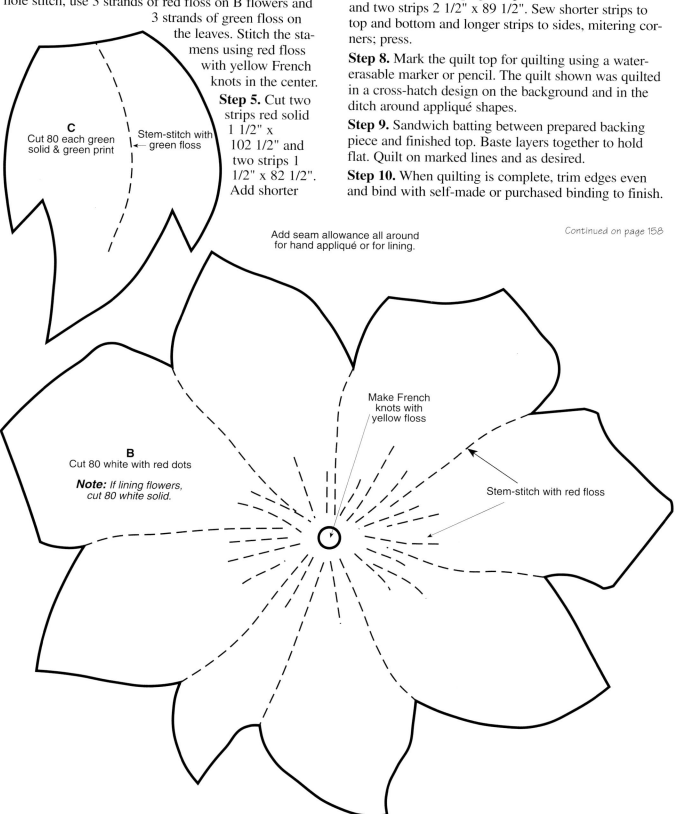

C
Cut 80 each green solid & green print

Stem-stitch with green floss

Add seam allowance all around for hand appliqué or for lining.

B
Cut 80 white with red dots

Note: *If lining flowers, cut 80 white solid.*

Make French knots with yellow floss

Stem-stitch with red floss

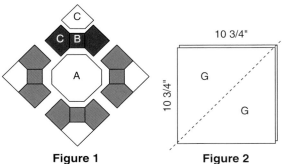

BOW-TIE WREATH QUILT

By Helen King & Eunice Plucknett

Use a variation of the traditional Bow Tie pattern to create a wreath design for a pretty Christmas quilt to treasure for years to come.

Making a quilt for use only during the holiday season may seem like a waste of time for some people, but we quilters like to decorate every room in the house with quilts.

Can you find the Bow Tie design in the wreaths on this pretty quilt? The center A piece replaces the C piece which would make four sections out of this block. If you prefer making four smaller blocks and joining them with seams in the center, replace the A piece with C pieces.

Project Specifications
Skill Level: Intermediate
Quilt Size: Approximately 73 1/4" x 93"
Block Size: 14" x 14"

Materials
- 5 yards muslin
- 5 yards green Christmas print
- 1 1/2 yards red Christmas print
- Backing 77" x 97"
- Batting 77" x 97"
- All purpose threads to match fabrics
- Water-erasable marker or pencil
- 10 yards self-made or purchased binding

Bow-Tie Wreath
14" x 14" Block

Traditional Method
Step 1. Prepare templates using pattern pieces given. Cut fabric patches as directed on each piece for the block.

Step 2. To piece one block, sew a print C to two opposite sides of B; set in a muslin C on one remaining side. Repeat for four units; set the units onto A to com-

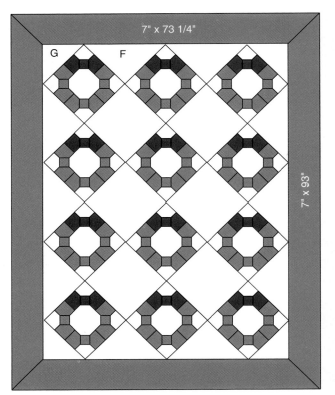

Bow-Tie Wreath
Placement Diagram
73 1/4" x 93"

plete one block referring to Figure 1. Repeat for 12 blocks; press.

Step 3. Cut six squares muslin 14 1/2" x 14 1/2". Cut two squares 10 3/4" x 10 3/4"; cut once on the diagonal as shown in Figure 2 to make G corner triangles. You will need four G triangles.

Figure 1
Sew pieces together as shown to piece 1 block.

Figure 2
Cut 2 squares on the diagonal to make G corner triangles.

Step 4. Cut three squares muslin 21" x 21"; cut on both diagonals as shown in Figure 3 to make F triangles. You will need 10 F triangles.

Step 5. Arrange the pieced blocks with the muslin squares and the F and G triangles in diagonal rows as shown in Figure 4. Join in rows; join the rows to complete quilt center; press.

Step 6. Measure the pieced top through the center both horizontally and vertically. Cut 7 1/2"-wide border strips these lengths, plus 14 1/2". Sew the short strips to the top and bottom and the longer strips to each side, mitering corners; press seams toward strips.

Step 7. Choose a pretty quilting pattern for the center

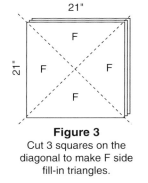

Figure 3
Cut 3 squares on the diagonal to make F side fill-in triangles.

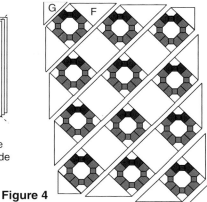

Figure 4
Arrange the pieced blocks, muslin squares and F and G triangles in diagonal rows.

square and F and G triangles. Mark the chosen design on the completed top using a water-erasable marker or pen.

Step 8. Sandwich batting between completed top and prepared backing piece. Pin or baste layers together to hold flat. Quilt as desired by hand or machine.

Step 9. When quilting is complete, remove pins or basting and trim edges even. Bind with self-made or purchased binding.

Quick Method

Step 1. For B squares, cut one red and three green fabric strips 2 3/4" by fabric width. Cut each strip into 2 3/4" squares; set aside.

Step 2. To make C-C bow units, cut 11 strips green and three strips red 4" by fabric width. Sew three red/green strips and four green/green strips. Make a template using fold line marked on C. Place this template on strips; cut out shapes.

Step 3. Cut five strips muslin 4" by fabric width; place C piece on each strip; trace. Cut apart on traced lines.

Step 4. Cut two strips muslin 7 1/2" by fabric width for A. Place A template on strips; trace. Cut apart on traced lines.

Step 5. To piece block, sew muslin C's to B; join with C-C units around A in a clockwise direction. Repeat for 12 blocks.

Step 6. Sew blocks together as for Traditional Method Steps 3–9.

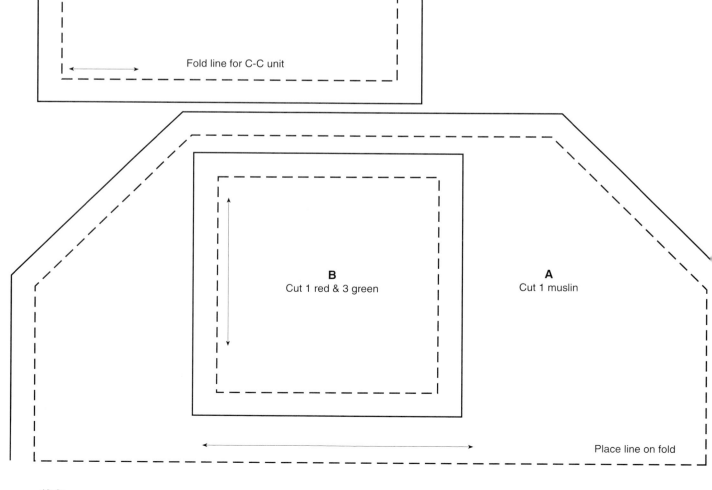

C
Cut 4 muslin, 2 red & 6 green

Fold line for C-C unit

B
Cut 1 red & 3 green

A
Cut 1 muslin

Place line on fold

PLAIDS FOR CHRISTMAS

By Sandra L. Hatch

Log Cabin quilts are fun to make. Even though this quilt is made with red and green plaid fabrics, the colors would fit into many room decorating schemes all year long!

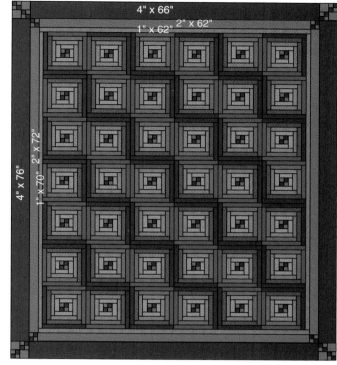

Plaids for Christmas
Placement Diagram
74" x 84"

Are you one of those people who cannot stand it if something isn't perfectly straight? Printed plaids drive you crazy because you have to make a choice—cut straight on the stripe or straight on the grain? If so, you probably don't use plaids in many of your quilts.

I didn't either until recently. For this Log Cabin quilt in red and green plaids, I found that you don't have to sew perfectly on every line to make the blocks work and that cutting plaids isn't so hard.

If you don't mind making a few extra blocks, try making a matching table runner or two. Make one with three or four blocks with several borders to place on your dresser during the holiday season.

Project Specifications
Skill Level: Intermediate
Quilt Size: 74" x 84"
Block Size: 10" x 10"
Number of Blocks: 42

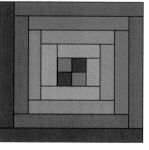

Log Cabin
10" x 10" Block

Materials
- 2 1/2 yards each #4 red and #3 and #4 green plaids
- 2 1/4 yards each #2 and #3 red and #2 green plaids
- 1/2 yard each #1 red and green plaids
- 2 spools all-purpose thread to match fabrics
- 1 spool red quilting thread
- Backing 78" x 88"
- Cotton batting 78" x 88"
- 9 yards self-made or purchased binding

Instructions
Step 1. Cut two strips each from #4 red and #3 green plaid fabrics 1 1/2" by the length (not across width) of each fabric piece for center Four-Patch units. *Note: It is easy to cut strips using shears and following lines on the plaids as guides.* Set aside.

Step 2. Cut four border strips from #4 red 4 1/2" by fabric length. Cut four strips #3 green 2 1/2" by fabric length and four strips #2 red 1 1/2" by fabric length. Set aside for borders.

Step 3. All fabric strips are cut 1 1/2" wide by the length of the yardage. From the yardage given in the list of materials, cut the following number of strips from each fabric: #1 green—15; #1 red—17; #2 green—seven; #2 red—eight; #3 green—nine; #3 red—10; #4 green—nine; #4 red—10. Set remaining

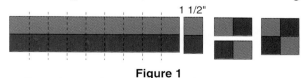

Figure 1
Sew strips together; cut apart in 1 1/2" segments. Resew segments to make Four-Patch center squares.

fabric aside for another project or for more strips if needed.

Step 4. Using strips cut in Step 1, sew a #4 red strip to a #3 green strip twice. Press seam toward red. Cut each strip into 1 1/2" segments. Repeat with two more strips to complete 108 segments. Resew the segments to make 54 Four-Patch squares for centers and borders as shown in Figure 1. Set aside 12 for border units.

Step 5. Piece 42 blocks referring to Figure 2 for order and color placement, using Four-Patch units as the center for each block. Sew all Four-Patch centers to a green #1 strip as shown in Figure 3. When stitching is complete, press seam toward strip; trim strip even with Four-Patch center as shown in Figure 4. Continue adding the pieced units to strips, pressing and trimming after each addition until you have added four logs to each side of the center unit. ***Note:*** *During assembly, stop about halfway through and check the size of the blocks. Square up and continue adding strips.*

Step 6. Press all blocks and square up to 10 1/2" x 10 1/2".

Step 7. Arrange the blocks in rows referring to the Placement Diagram for Straight Furrow arrangement of the Log Cabin blocks.

Step 8. Sew the blocks in rows; join the rows to complete the pieced center.

Step 9. From previously cut border strips, cut two red #2 strips 1 1/2" x 70 1/2". Sew to long sides of the quilt center; press. Cut two more strips 1 1/2" x 62 1/2" and sew to top and bottom; press.

Step 10. From the previously cut border strips, cut two strips #3 green 2 1/2" x 72 1/2" and sew to quilt sides. Cut two more strips 2 1/2" x 62 1/2". Sew a Four-Patch unit to each end of each strip and sew to top and bottom referring to the Placement Diagram for arrangement of Four-Patch units; press.

Step 11. Cut eight 2 1/2" x 2 1/2" squares from green #3. Sew two of these squares together with two Four-Patch units to make squares for corners as shown in Figure 5.

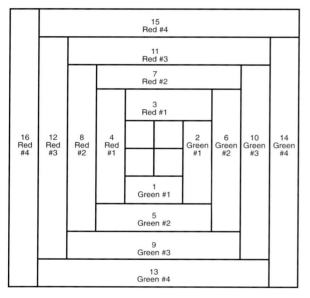

Figure 2
Piece 42 blocks in color and
numerical order shown.

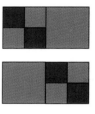

Figure 5
Sew squares to Four-Patch units
as shown. Sew resulting units
together to make larger
Four-Patch units for corners.

Figure 3
Sew a Four-Patch unit
to a green #1 strip.

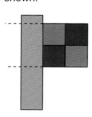

Figure 4
Trim strip even with
Four-Patch unit.

Step 12. Cut two red #4 strips 4 1/2" x 76 1/2" and sew to quilt sides; press. Cut two more strips 4 1/2" x 66 1/2". Sew a large Four-Patch unit to the ends of each strip referring to the Placement Diagram for arrangement of Four-Patch units. Sew to top and bottom to complete quilt top. Press.

Step 13. Sandwich batting between completed top and prepared backing piece. Baste or pin layers together to hold flat.

Step 14. Quilt as desired by hand or machine.

Step 15. When quilting is complete, trim edges even. Remove basting or pins. Bind with self-made or purchased binding to finish.

WHERE'S RUDOLPH?

By Lisa Christensen

Can you find Rudolph in this wall hanging? He is easy to spot if you look for the right thing!

The technique used to make this pieced wall hanging uses squares and rectangles to create triangle shapes. Layering a square on the end of another square and stitching across the diagonal creates a triangle corner when the stitched square is folded back. The extra layers underneath may be trimmed away for hand quilting or left to add stability to the blocks during the construction process.

Project Specifications
Skill Level: Intermediate
Wall Hanging Size: 27 1/2" x 39"
Block Size: 5 1/2" x 7"

Materials
- 1 fat quarter brown print for reindeer bodies and tree trunks
- 1 fat quarter tan print for body contrast
- Scraps gold print for collars and red print for nose
- 1 fat quarter green print for trees
- 1/4 yard green print for inside border
- 3/4 yard black holiday print for outside border
- 1 yard white-on-white print for background
- 1 spool neutral color all-purpose thread
- 1 spool choice of quilting thread
- Batting 30" x 42"
- Backing 30" x 42"
- 4 yards self-made or purchased binding

Instructions
Step 1. Referring to Figure 1 for cutting, cut pieces for one reindeer; repeat for nine reindeer—one with a red nose—as shown in Figure 2.

Step 2. Refer to Figure 2 drawings to complete one reindeer block; repeat for nine blocks. *Note: Make one reindeer with a red nose referring to Figure 3 for changes in piecing.* Press and square up blocks to 6" x 7 1/2".

Step 3. Referring to Figure 4 for cutting, cut pieces for one tree block; repeat for three blocks.

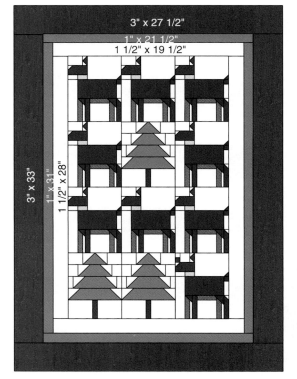

Where's Rudolph?
Placement Diagram
27 1/2" x 39"

Step 4. Refer to Figure 5 drawings to complete one tree block; repeat for three blocks. Press and square up blocks to 6" x 7 1/2".

Step 5. Arrange the pieced blocks in four rows of three blocks each referring to the Placement Diagram for placement of trees and reindeer. Join the blocks in rows; join the rows to complete the quilt center; press.

Step 6. Cut two strips first border white-on-white 2" x 28 1/2"; sew a strip to each long side. Cut two more strips 2" x 20"; sew a strip to the top and bottom. Press seams toward strips.

Step 7. Cut two strips green print 1 1/2" x 31 1/2"; sew a strip to each long side. Cut two more strips 1 1/2" x 22"; sew a strip to the top and bottom. Press seams toward strips.

Step 8. Cut two strips black print 3 1/2" x 33 1/2": sew a strip to each long side. Cut two more strips 3 1/2" x 28"; sew a strip to the top and bottom. Press seams toward strips.

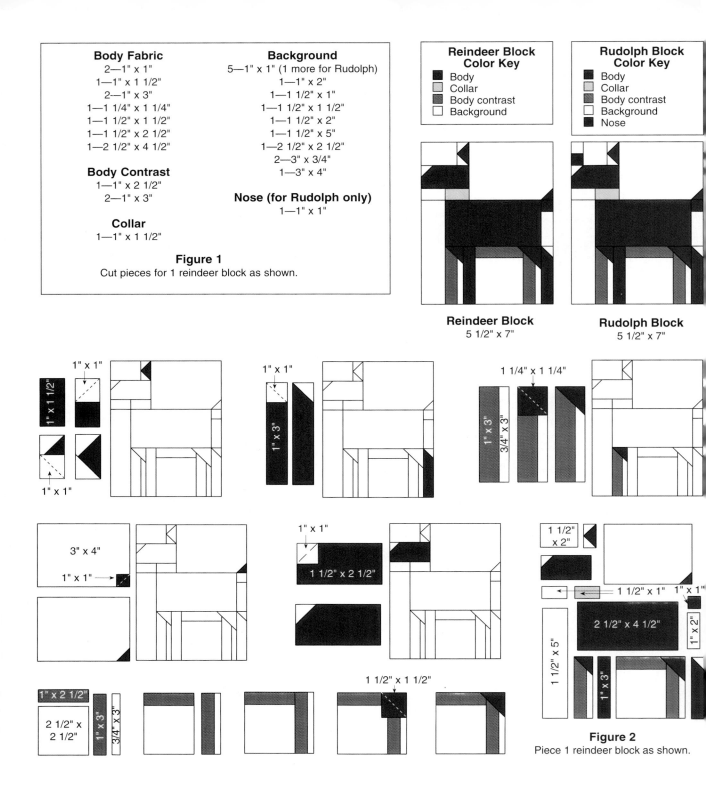

Body Fabric
2—1" x 1"
1—1" x 1 1/2"
2—1" x 3"
1—1 1/4" x 1 1/4"
1—1 1/2" x 1 1/2"
1—1 1/2" x 2 1/2"
1—2 1/2" x 4 1/2"

Body Contrast
1—1" x 2 1/2"
2—1" x 3"

Collar
1—1" x 1 1/2"

Background
5—1" x 1" (1 more for Rudolph)
1—1" x 2"
1—1 1/2" x 1"
1—1 1/2" x 1 1/2"
1—1 1/2" x 2"
1—1 1/2" x 5"
1—2 1/2" x 2 1/2"
2—3" x 3/4"
1—3" x 4"

Nose (for Rudolph only)
1—1" x 1"

Figure 1
Cut pieces for 1 reindeer block as shown.

Reindeer Block Color Key
Body
Collar
Body contrast
Background

Rudolph Block Color Key
Body
Collar
Body contrast
Background
Nose

Reindeer Block
5 1/2" x 7"

Rudolph Block
5 1/2" x 7"

Figure 2
Piece 1 reindeer block as shown.

Step 9. Sandwich batting between the completed top and prepared backing piece. Pin or baste layers together to hold flat.

Step 10. Machine-quilt in the ditch of the seams and as desired. When quilting is complete, trim edges even. Bind with self-made or purchased binding to finish.

Rudolph's nose
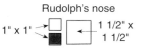
1" x 1"
1 1/2" x 1 1/2"

Figure 3
Piece 1 reindeer block with red nose as shown.

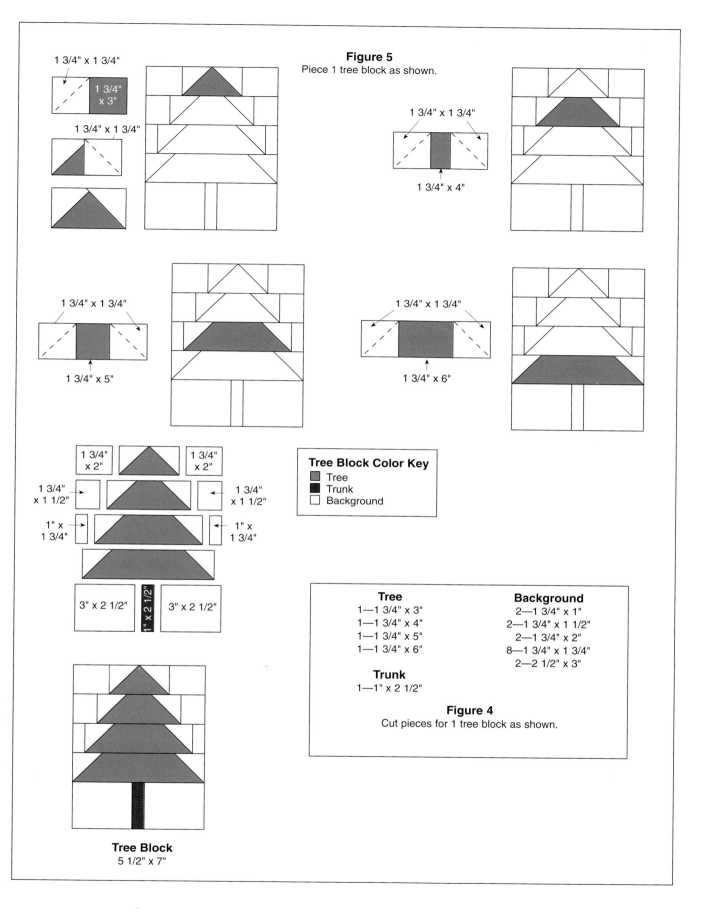

Figure 5
Piece 1 tree block as shown.

1 3/4" x 1 3/4"

1 3/4" x 3"

1 3/4" x 1 3/4"

1 3/4" x 1 3/4"

1 3/4" x 4"

1 3/4" x 1 3/4"

1 3/4" x 5"

1 3/4" x 1 3/4"

1 3/4" x 6"

1 3/4" x 2"

1 3/4" x 2"

1 3/4" x 1 1/2"

1 3/4" x 1 1/2"

1" x 1 3/4"

1" x 1 3/4"

3" x 2 1/2"

1" x 2 1/2"

3" x 2 1/2"

Tree Block Color Key
- Tree
- Trunk
- Background

Tree
1—1 3/4" x 3"
1—1 3/4" x 4"
1—1 3/4" x 5"
1—1 3/4" x 6"

Trunk
1—1" x 2 1/2"

Background
2—1 3/4" x 1"
2—1 3/4" x 1 1/2"
2—1 3/4" x 2"
8—1 3/4" x 1 3/4"
2—2 1/2" x 3"

Figure 4
Cut pieces for 1 tree block as shown.

Tree Block
5 1/2" x 7"

CABIN FEVER SANTA

By Sue Harvey

I have been collecting old holiday postcards for several years. The inspiration for this Santa came from a card postmarked 1907. Because old Santas usually have a gold tassel at the end of their stocking hats, I gave my Santa a gold pompon as a bridge between the old and new.

After I completed this wall hanging, the name *Cabin Fever Santa* popped into my head. When the hectic Christmas season is over, I can imagine Mr. and Mrs. Claus spending the rest of every winter cooped up in their little North Pole cabin anxiously awaiting that first day of spring!

Project Specifications
Skill Level: Intermediate
Quilt Size: 34" x 34"

Materials
- 7/8 yard red/green plaid
- 1 fat quarter each red solid, white/red print, red/black print, red/white print and red print #1
- 1/3 yard red print #2 for blocks and borders
- Scraps of dark green and red for holly leaves and berries
- Scraps of red plaid, ecru, gold, skin tone, dark blue, wine, plum, and green and white-on-white prints for Santa appliqué
- Backing 38" x 38"
- Batting 38" x 38"
- 1 skein dark taupe embroidery floss
- All-purpose threads to match fabrics
- 1 spool quilting thread
- 4 1/2 yards self-made or purchased binding

Pieced Section
Step 1. Cut the pieces for the Log Cabin half-blocks as indicated in the Cutting Chart.

Step 2. Add a red/green plaid C triangle to one end of all even-length log pieces as shown in Figure 1; press seam toward C. Add a red/green plaid C to one end of all odd-length log pieces as shown in Figure 2; press seams toward C.

Cabin Fever Santa
Placement Diagram
34" x 34"

Cutting Chart
Red/green plaid—1 square 19" x 19"; 8 B and 40 C
Red solid—4 A
White/red print—4 strips 1 1/2" x 3 1/2"; 4 strips 1 1/2" x 4 1/2"
Red/white print—4 strips 1 1/2" x 5 1/2"; 4 strips 1 1/2" x 6 1/2"
Red print #1—4 strips 1 1/2" x 7 1/2"; 4 strips 1 1/2" x 8 1/2"
Red print #2—4 strips 1 1/2" x 9 1/2"; 4 strips 1 1/2" x 10 1/2"
Red/black print—4 strips 1 1/2" x 11 1/2"; 4 strips 1 1/2" x 12 1/2"

Step 3. Add a red/green plaid B triangle to two adjacent sides of a red solid A square as shown in Figure 3. Press seams toward B triangles; repeat three times.

Step 4. To piece the Log Cabin half-blocks, sew one white/red print 1 1/2" x 3 1/2" C log unit to the B-A-

Figure 1
Add a red/green plaid C triangle to 1 end of all even-length log pieces as shown.

Figure 2
Add a red/green plaid C triangle to 1 end of all odd-length log pieces as shown.

B triangle unit as shown in Figure 4; press the seam toward the log unit. Sew one white/red print 1 1/2" x 4 1/2" C log unit to the B-A-B log unit as shown in Figure 5; press seam toward the log unit.

Step 5. Continue to add log units, ending with a red/black print 1 1/2" x 12 1/2" C log unit to complete the Log Cabin half-block as shown in Figure 6.

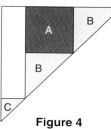

Figure 3
Add a red/green plaid B triangle to 2 adjacent sides of a red solid A square.

Figure 4
Sew 1 white/red print 1 1/2" x 3 1/2" C log unit to the B-A-B triangle unit.

Log unit

Figure 5
Sew 1 white/red print 1 1/2" x 3 1/2" C log unit to the B-A-B log unit.

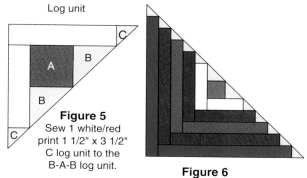

Figure 6
Continue to add log units, ending with the red/black print 1 1/2" x 12 1/2" C log unit to complete the Log Cabin half-block.

Step 6. Repeat Steps 4 and 5 to piece three more Log Cabin half-blocks.

Step 7. Place a long ruler on the C triangle edge of each block; line up the 1/4" mark with the outer corner of each log; trim the block edge as shown in Figure 7 if necessary, leaving a 1/4" seam allowance.

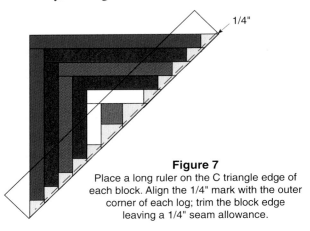

1/4"

Figure 7
Place a long ruler on the C triangle edge of each block. Align the 1/4" mark with the outer corner of each log; trim the block edge leaving a 1/4" seam allowance.

Step 8. Sew one Log Cabin half-block to each side of the 19" x 19" red/green plaid square.

Step 9. Cut two strips red/green plaid 2" x 26 1/2"; sew a strip to each side of the pieced top; trim and press seams toward the border strip. Cut two strips red/green plaid 2" x 29 1/2"; sew a strip to the top and bottom of the pieced top; trim and press seams toward border strips.

Step 10. Cut two strips 3" x 29 1/2" red print #2; sew a strip to each side of the pieced top; trim and press seams toward border strip. Cut two strips 3" x 34 1/2" red print #2; sew a strip to the top and bottom of the pieced top; trim and press seams toward border strips.

Appliqué Instructions

Step 1. Make templates for each part of the Santa; cut out one of each piece from the appropriate fabrics as noted on the Santa pattern and referring to the Placement Diagram, adding 1/4" seam allowance to each piece when cutting for hand appliqué. *Note: Cut each piece to allow for the portion that will be under an adjacent piece as indicated by the dotted lines on the pattern.* Turn under the 1/4" seam allowance on each piece (except where another piece overlaps a piece); baste in place.

Step 2. Mark templates for the holly leaves and berries; cut as directed on each piece, adding a 1/4" seam allowance to fabric pieces when cutting.

Step 3. Fold the pieced top in half vertically and horizontally; crease on the fold lines to mark centers.

Step 4. Place the face piece (1) on the top, lining up the top center with the center of the pattern piece (marked with an X). Appliqué in place, leaving the left edge open in order to slide the beard piece (2) underneath.

Step 5. Place the white beard piece (2) on the top; slip the left edge under the face piece (1) and the inner right edge over the face piece (1) as shown on the pattern. Appliqué in place, leaving a section of the right side edge and the right bottom edge open in order to slide the red plaid suit pieces (8 and 9) underneath.

Step 6. Continue to appliqué the Santa pieces in place in numerical order, being careful to leave edges open

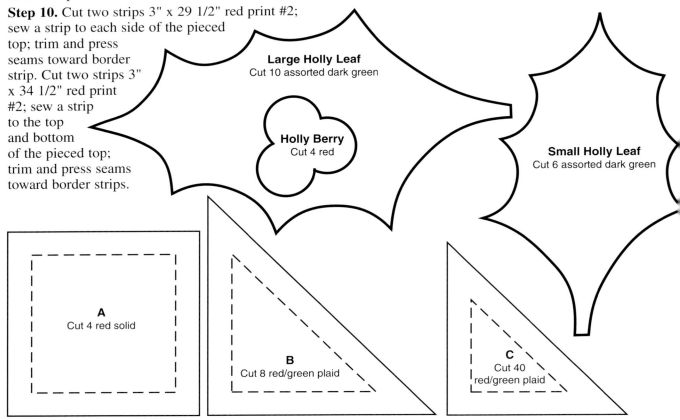

Large Holly Leaf
Cut 10 assorted dark green

Holly Berry
Cut 4 red

Small Holly Leaf
Cut 6 assorted dark green

A
Cut 4 red solid

B
Cut 8 red/green plaid

C
Cut 40 red/green plaid

for overlapping pieces where indicated on the pattern.

Step 7. Embroider the nose line and the two eye lines using the dark taupe embroidery floss as shown on the Santa pattern.

Step 8. Appliqué the holly leaves and berries in place in the center of each outer side of the pieced top referring to the Placement Diagram.

Finishing the Quilt

Step 1. Mark the top for quilting as desired using a water-erasable pencil or marker. The sample was outline-quilted around each appliquéd piece and in straight lines radiating from the Santa to the outside edges and corners.

Step 2. Sandwich batting between the completed top and prepared backing piece. Pin or baste layers together to hold flat.

Step 3. Quilt on marked lines and as desired by hand or machine.

Step 4. When quilting is complete, trim edges even. Bind with self-made or purchased binding to finish.

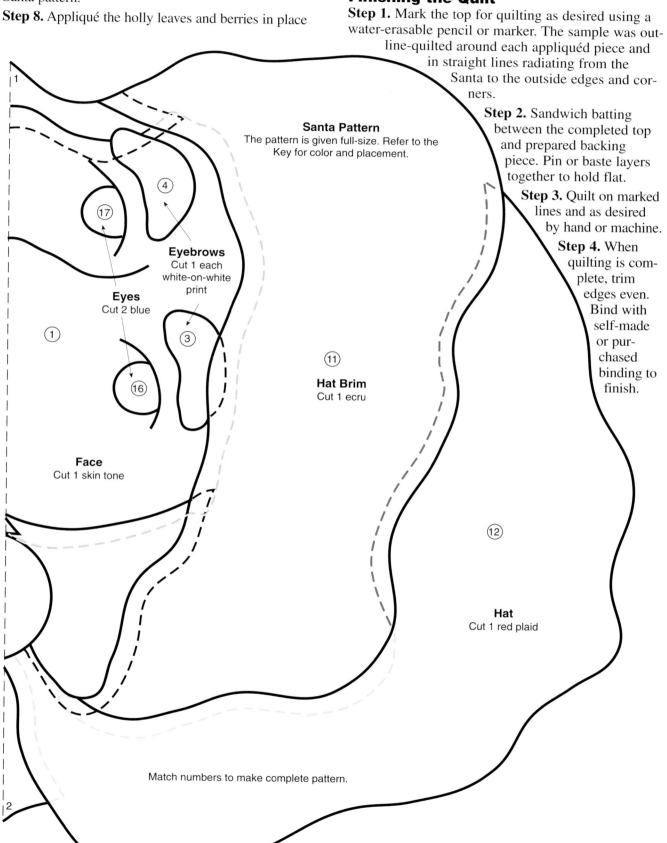

Santa Pattern
The pattern is given full-size. Refer to the Key for color and placement.

4

17

Eyebrows
Cut 1 each
white-on-white
print

Eyes
Cut 2 blue

1

3

16

11

Hat Brim
Cut 1 ecru

Face
Cut 1 skin tone

12

Hat
Cut 1 red plaid

Match numbers to make complete pattern.

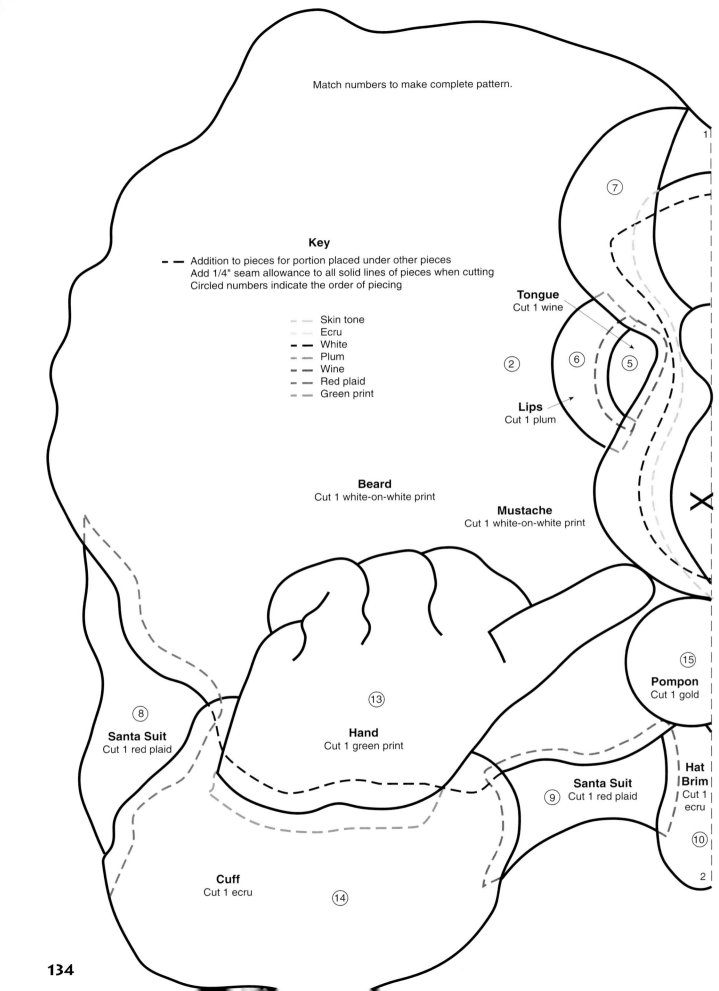

Match numbers to make complete pattern.

Key

– — Addition to pieces for portion placed under other pieces
Add 1/4" seam allowance to all solid lines of pieces when cutting
Circled numbers indicate the order of piecing

- Skin tone
- Ecru
- White
- Plum
- Wine
- Red plaid
- Green print

Tongue
Cut 1 wine

Lips
Cut 1 plum

Beard
Cut 1 white-on-white print

Mustache
Cut 1 white-on-white print

Pompon
Cut 1 gold

Santa Suit
Cut 1 red plaid

Hand
Cut 1 green print

Santa Suit
Cut 1 red plaid

Hat Brim
Cut 1 ecru

Cuff
Cut 1 ecru

THE OTHER CHRISTMAS STARS

By Connie Rand

Usually when we think of stars at Christmastime, the great star that guided the wise men to Jesus' birthplace comes to mind. That star dominated the night sky then, but there was a multitude of other stars, each testifying to the power of the Creator. This quilt is full of small stars, in recognition of His infinite glory.

This quilt looks difficult, but the small stars are really not so hard to piece, and squares make up the rest of the design. Color placement is very important to the overall look of the finished quilt. Refer to the Placement Diagram and the block piecing diagram to achieve perfect results.

Project Specifications
Skill Level: Intermediate
Block Size: 12" x 12"
Quilt Size: 59" x 83"

Materials
- 2 1/2 yards yellow print
- 2 1/2 yards blue-and-gold metallic print
- 2/3 yard red solid
- 1/2 yard dark green print #1
- 2 1/2 yards dark green print #2
- 1/2 yard light green print
- Backing 63" x 87"
- Batting 63" x 87"
- 8 1/2 yards self-made or purchased binding

Instructions
Step 1. Prepare templates using pattern pieces given. Cut fabric patches as directed on each piece to complete 24 blocks.

Step 2. To piece one block, sew B and BR to C. Sew F

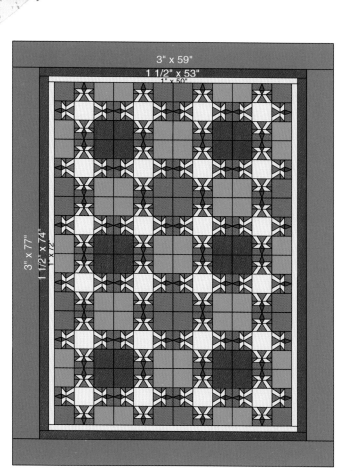

The Other Christmas Stars
Placement Diagram
59" x 83"

The Other Christmas Stars
12" x 12" Block

to E and FR to ER; join with D. Sew H to G and HR to GR; join with I. Join these row units as shown in Figure 1 to complete one star unit; press. Complete four star units for each block.

Step 3. Arrange the pieced star units with A in rows as shown in Figure 2, referring to Placement

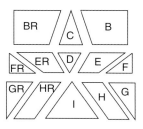

Figure 1
Piece star units as shown.

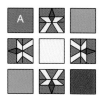

Figure 2
Arrange star units with A in rows to make 1 block.

Diagram for color placement. Join together to complete one block; repeat for 24 blocks.

Step 4. Arrange the completed blocks in six rows of four blocks each referring to the Placement Diagram. Join in rows; join rows to complete the top; press.

Step 5. Cut two yellow print border strips 1 1/2" x 72 1/2"; sew to long sides of quilt center. Cut two more strips 1 1/2" x 50 1/2"; sew to top and bottom; press.

Step 6. Cut two red solid border strips 2" x 74 1/2"; sew to long sides of quilt center. Cut two more strips 2" x 53 1/2"; sew to top and bottom; press.

Step 7. Cut two green print #2 border strips 3 1/2" x 77 1/2"; sew to long sides of quilt center. Cut two more strips 3 1/2" x 59 1/2"; sew to top and bottom; press.

Step 8. Sandwich batting between completed top and prepared backing piece. Baste or pin layers together to hold flat for quilting.

Step 9. Quilt in the ditch of the seams of each block and border strips or as desired by hand or machine.

Step 10. When quilting is complete, trim edges even and remove basting or pins.

Step 11. Bind edges with self-made or purchased binding to finish.

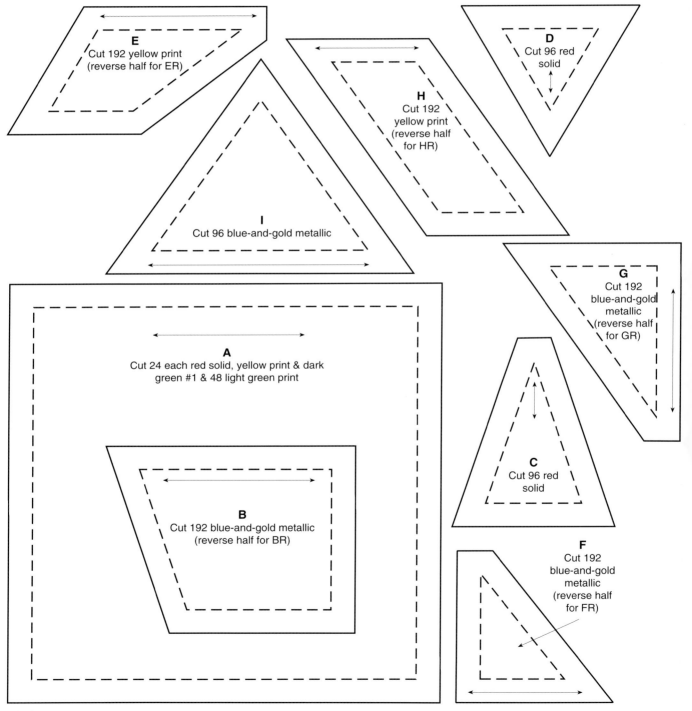

E
Cut 192 yellow print
(reverse half for ER)

D
Cut 96 red solid

H
Cut 192 yellow print
(reverse half for HR)

I
Cut 96 blue-and-gold metallic

G
Cut 192 blue-and-gold metallic
(reverse half for GR)

A
Cut 24 each red solid, yellow print & dark green #1 & 48 light green print

B
Cut 192 blue-and-gold metallic
(reverse half for BR)

C
Cut 96 red solid

F
Cut 192 blue-and-gold metallic
(reverse half for FR)

GIFT BRINGER SANTA

By Marian Shenk

If you like old-fashioned Santas, you'll love this appliquéd wall hanging. Santa is laden with gifts and ready to start on his gift-giving journey.

Here is your chance to have some fun using embellishments wherever you want. Add trims to Santa's sack or the toys or decorate the tree using embellishments of your choice.

Although the project shown was hand-appliquéd, you may wish to create a quicker project using machine appliqué. For machine appliqué add a seam allowance to pieces only on sides where they are overlapped by another appliqué piece.

Project Specifications
Skill Level: Advanced
Quilt Size: 26" x 31"

Materials
- 3/4 yard beige-on-beige print for background
- 1 piece white-on-white print 7" x 18"
- 1/4 yard red print for first border
- 1 yard border stripe
- 1 package green 1/2"-wide bias tape
- 1/4 yard red velour
- Scraps of fake fur for beard and coat trim
- Fabric scraps for gloves, boots, toys in sack, sack and signpost
- Scrap white felt for mustache and eyebrows
- 1/4 yard green print for tree and holly
- Assortment of beads for tree, berries and holly trim, gold star for tree and black cord for Santa's belt
- Metallic threads, ribbon and embroidery floss for embellishments
- Backing 28" x 34"
- Batting 28" x 34
- 3 1/4 yards self-made or purchased binding
- Water-erasable marker or pencil

Instructions
Step 1. Cut a piece of background fabric 18" x 23". Fold and crease to mark center.

Step 2. Copy and join the four sections of the full-size pattern to create one large pattern. Trace around edges

Gift Bringer Santa
Placement Diagram
26" x 31"

with a dark marker to make lines darker; mark center. Tape the pattern to a light source. ***Note:*** *A large window will also work.*

Step 3. Center the background piece over the drawing, matching centers; secure in place. Trace the drawing onto the background fabric using a very light pencil

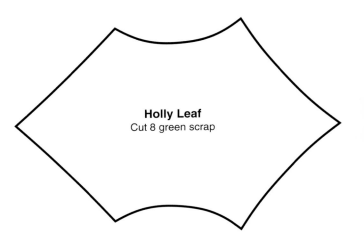

Holly Leaf
Cut 8 green scrap

line or water-erasable marker. Transfer numbers indicating order of appliqué to background.

Step 4. Separate the paper pattern and the background. Cut out each shape from the paper pattern. Choose fabric scraps for each shape.

Step 5. Cut each shape from chosen fabric scraps, adding a 1/8" to 1/4" seam allowance to each piece.

Step 6. Pin and appliqué pieces to background in numerical order, turning edges under when stitching. **Note:** *Do not turn edges under on edges of pieces* *where another piece overlaps.*

Step 7. Cut two strips red print 2 1/4" x 21 1/2" and two strips 2 1/4" x 26 1/2". Sew short strips to the top and bottom and long strips to sides, mitering corners; press seams toward strips.

Step 8. Cut two strips stripe fabric 3" x 26 1/2" and two strips 3" x 31 1/2". Sew short strips to the top and bottom and long strips to sides, mitering corners; press seams toward strips.

Step 9. Cut two pieces of bias tape 20" long and two pieces 25" long. Place short pieces next to red border strip on the top and bottom and long pieces on the sides; appliqué in place, trimming and mitering at corners.

Step 10. Embellish tree with beads and metallic thread stitches; sew large star to the top. Unstitch a small spot on the belt and insert cording; secure. Add beads or embroidery for berries on hat. Use fake fur for horse's mane; make a bow on bear's neck using ribbon or embroidery floss. Embroider signpost directions using a stem stitch.

Step 11. Appliqué holly leaves in place at red border corners. Sew three red beads in place for berries.

Step 12. Sandwich batting between the completed top and the prepared backing piece; pin or baste layers together to hold flat.

Step 13. Echo-quilt around shapes and as desired on background and borders.

Step 14. When quilting is complete, remove basting or pins; trim edges even.

Step 15. Bind edges with self-made or purchased binding to finish.

Signs
Cut 1 each
brown
scrap

Signpost
Cut 1
brown
scrap

Hand
Cut 1 black scrap
(1 piece tucked under
stick and folded over)

Pole
Cut 1 brown sc

Match numbers at corners to make
full-size pattern drawing.

⑦ ⑤ ⑥ ⑨ ⑧

4

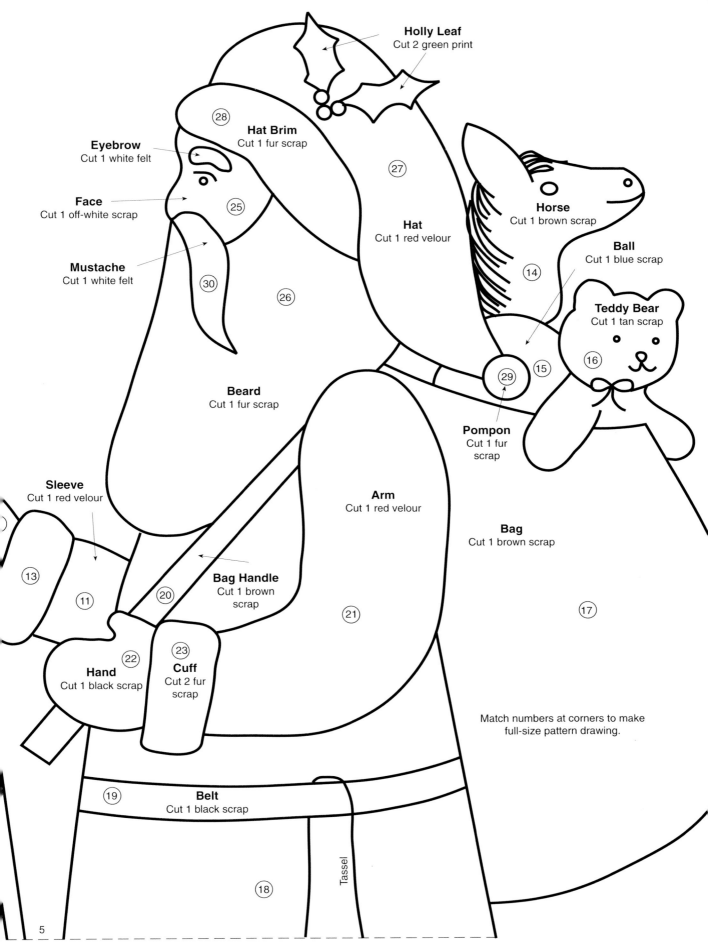

Holly Leaf
Cut 2 green print

(28)

Hat Brim
Cut 1 fur scrap

(27)

Eyebrow
Cut 1 white felt

(25)

Hat
Cut 1 red velour

Horse
Cut 1 brown scrap

Face
Cut 1 off-white scrap

Ball
Cut 1 blue scrap

(14)

Mustache
Cut 1 white felt

(30)

(26)

Teddy Bear
Cut 1 tan scrap

(29)

(15)

(16)

Beard
Cut 1 fur scrap

Pompon
Cut 1 fur
scrap

Sleeve
Cut 1 red velour

Arm
Cut 1 red velour

Bag
Cut 1 brown scrap

(13)

(11)

(20)

Bag Handle
Cut 1 brown
scrap

(21)

(17)

(22)

(23)

Hand
Cut 1 black scrap

Cuff
Cut 2 fur
scrap

Match numbers at corners to make
full-size pattern drawing.

(19)

Belt
Cut 1 black scrap

Tassel

(18)

5

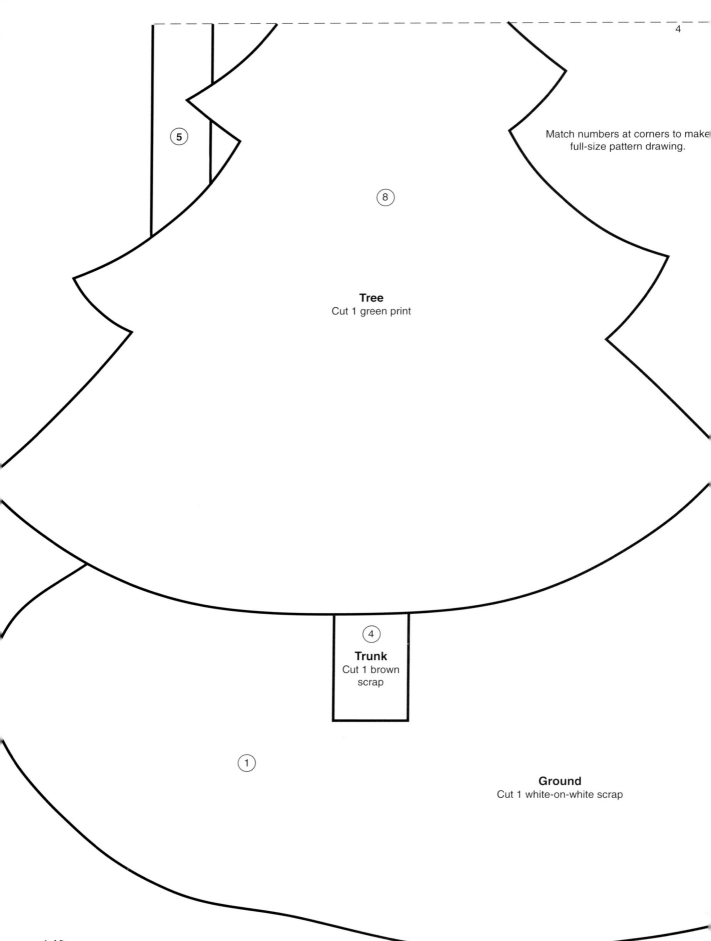

4

⑤

⑧

Match numbers at corners to make
full-size pattern drawing.

Tree
Cut 1 green print

④
Trunk
Cut 1 brown
scrap

①

Ground
Cut 1 white-on-white scrap

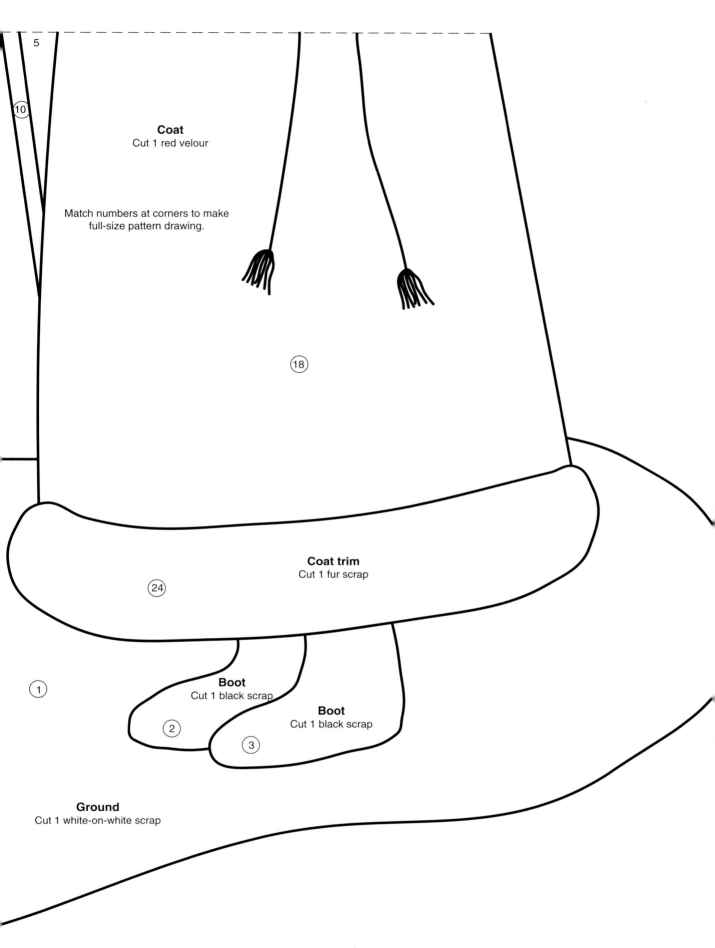

Coat
Cut 1 red velour

Match numbers at corners to make
full-size pattern drawing.

Coat trim
Cut 1 fur scrap

Boot
Cut 1 black scrap

Boot
Cut 1 black scrap

Ground
Cut 1 white-on-white scrap

ANTIQUE CAKE STAND QUILT

By Sue Harvey

I purchased this quilt at an antique auction in Fairfield, Maine. One of the solid setting squares is quilted with several sets of initials. It is not dated but appears to have been made around the turn of the century. Completed in Christmas colors, it makes a perfect holiday decoration.

Antique quilts can be duplicated in pattern, but the age factor, the feel or the look cannot be transferred to new fabrics and batting. You can come close, but you can't make a new quilt an antique.

Substitute popular colors in fabric prints of today, or use reproduction antique prints that will help to achieve the same look.

Project Specifications
Skill Level: Intermediate
Quilt Size: 77" x 89"
Block Size: 6" x 6"

Materials
- 1 1/4 yards green print
- 2 1/2 yards red print
- 5 yards white solid
- Backing 81" x 93"
- Batting 81" x 93"
- All-purpose threads to match fabrics
- 1 spool quilting thread
- 9 1/2 yards self-made or purchased binding

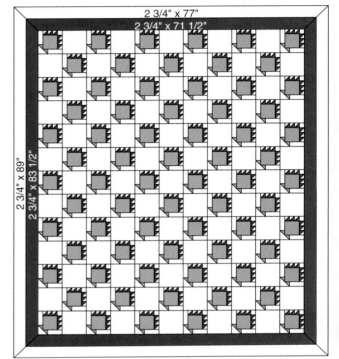

Antique Cake Stand
Placement Diagram
77" x 89"

Instructions
Step 1. Cut two strips red print 3 1/4" x 72" and two strips 3 1/4" x 84" for borders; set aside.

Step 2. Cut two strips white 3 1/4" x 77 1/2" and two strips 3 1/4" x 89 1/2" for borders; set aside.

Step 3. Prepare templates using pattern pieces given. Cut as directed on each piece to complete the quilt as shown.

Step 4. To piece one block, sew a white B to a red B six times. Join three B units twice. Arrange with

Cake Stand
6" x 6" Block

remaining pieces and join referring to Figure 1; repeat for 72 blocks; press.

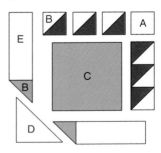

Figure 1
Join the pieces as shown to complete 1 block.

Step 5. Cut 71 squares white solid 6 1/2" x 6 1/2".

Step 6. Arrange the pieced blocks with the white squares in 13 horizontal rows referring to the Placement Diagram. Join the rows to complete the center pieced section; press.

Step 7. Sew the 3 1/4" x 72" red print strips to the top and bottom of the pieced center; sew the 3 1/4" x 84"

ANGEL HEART QUILT

By Nancy Brenan Daniel

How many times have you needed a really heavenly gift idea for that special friend or secret sister? Here is a quick quilt that will go together in an evening and will tell a special person just how you feel! This design may be adapted to make a smaller quilt or even a set of Christmas pot holders for the kitchen.

The Angel Heart design is quick and easy to cut and easy to stencil because you use freezer paper! The paper stencil is easy to use and dispose of after you finish stenciling.

The instructions are written for traditional piecing techniques, but if you are skilled in rapid-piecing techniques, you will find it very easy to adapt the measurements to create an even faster version of this heavenly quick *Angel Heart Quilt.*

Project Specifications:
Skill Level: Easy
Block Size: 7 1/2" x 7 1/2"
Quilt Size: Approximately 27 1/4" x 27 1/4"

Materials
- 1/2 yard Christmas print
- 1/3 yard muslin
- 1/4 yard dark green chintz
- Batting 30" x 30"
- Backing 31" x 31"
- Supplies: stencil paint and brush, freezer paper, paper scissors or craft knife

Instructions
Step 1. Cut fabrics for quilt as directed in Figure 1 and on piece D.

Step 2. Trace the Angel and large Heart designs onto the rough side of a piece of freezer paper, leaving several inches between the stencil designs.

Step 3. Carefully cut the designs from the paper, leaving the angel design space open. ***Note:*** *Do not cut away the paper from the angel or heart shapes; leave*

Angel Heart Quilt
Placement Diagram
27 1/4" x 27 1/4"

the design space open on the paper. The open negative area will be the stencil.

Step 4. Center the Angel stencil on one of the 8" x 8" squares. With a warm iron, press the freezer-paper stencil onto the fabric with the slick side down. Iron the cutout heart design in the center of the angel as shown in Figure 2. This covers the heart design space so the stencil paint won't cover it.

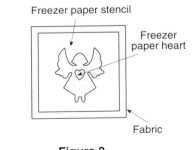

Figure 2
Iron freezer paper stencil to fabric and iron
cutout heart design in center of angel.

Step 5. Dip the stencil brush into the paint; wipe most of the paint out of the brush.

Step 6. Beginning from the outside, brush the paint

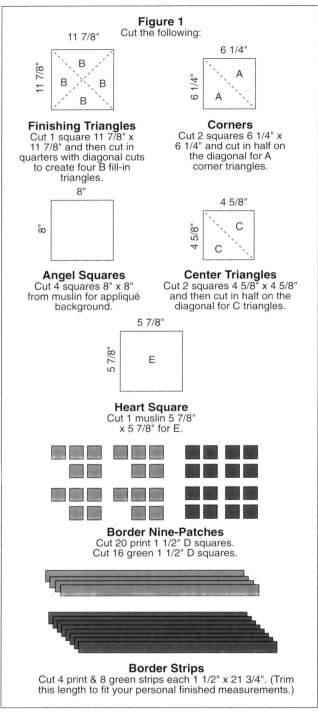

Figure 1
Cut the following:

11 7/8"

B
B   B
B

Finishing Triangles
Cut 1 square 11 7/8" x
11 7/8" and then cut in
quarters with diagonal cuts
to create four B fill-in
triangles.

6 1/4"
6 1/4"

A
A

Corners
Cut 2 squares 6 1/4" x
6 1/4" and cut in half on
the diagonal for A
corner triangles.

8"
8"

Angel Squares
Cut 4 squares 8" x 8"
from muslin for appliqué
background.

4 5/8"
4 5/8"

C
C

Center Triangles
Cut 2 squares 4 5/8" x 4 5/8"
and then cut in half on the
diagonal for C triangles.

5 7/8"
5 7/8"

E

Heart Square
Cut 1 muslin 5 7/8"
x 5 7/8" for E.

Border Nine-Patches
Cut 20 print 1 1/2" D squares.
Cut 16 green 1 1/2" D squares.

Border Strips
Cut 4 print & 8 green strips each 1 1/2" x 21 3/4". (Trim
this length to fit your personal finished measurements.)

until the total area is evenly covered with paint; repeat
this step for remaining Angels.

Step 7. Repeat stenciling steps for center Heart
block with large Heart design.

Step 8. Arrange stenciled blocks with A, B and C triangles referring to Figure 3; sew together in diagonal
rows. Join the rows to complete the center; press.

Borders

Step 1. Construct four Nine-Patch units using template
D or with strips cut as directed in Figure 1. Join

together to make border strip sets and Nine-Patch
blocks referring to Figure 4.

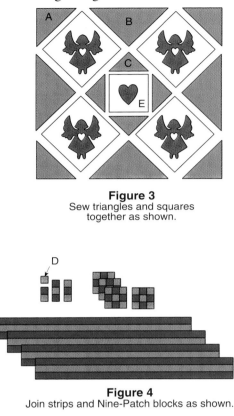

Figure 3
Sew triangles and squares
together as shown.

D

Figure 4
Join strips and Nine-Patch blocks as shown.

Figure 5
Add border strips to complete the top.

Step 2. Sew a border strip set to the top and bottom of
the quilt top center; trim excess fabric if necessary.

Step 3. Sew a Nine-Patch block to each end of the
remaining border strip sets; sew to quilt sides as shown
in Figure 5; press.

Step 4. Sandwich batting between completed top and
prepared backing piece. Pin or baste layers together to
hold flat.

Step 5. Quilt around each of the angels and the heart design and as desired.

Step 6. Trim batting only with quilt top edge. Trim backing piece 1" larger than quilt top all around. Turn under edge of backing 1/2"; pull over to right side of quilt top; hand-stitch in place to finish.

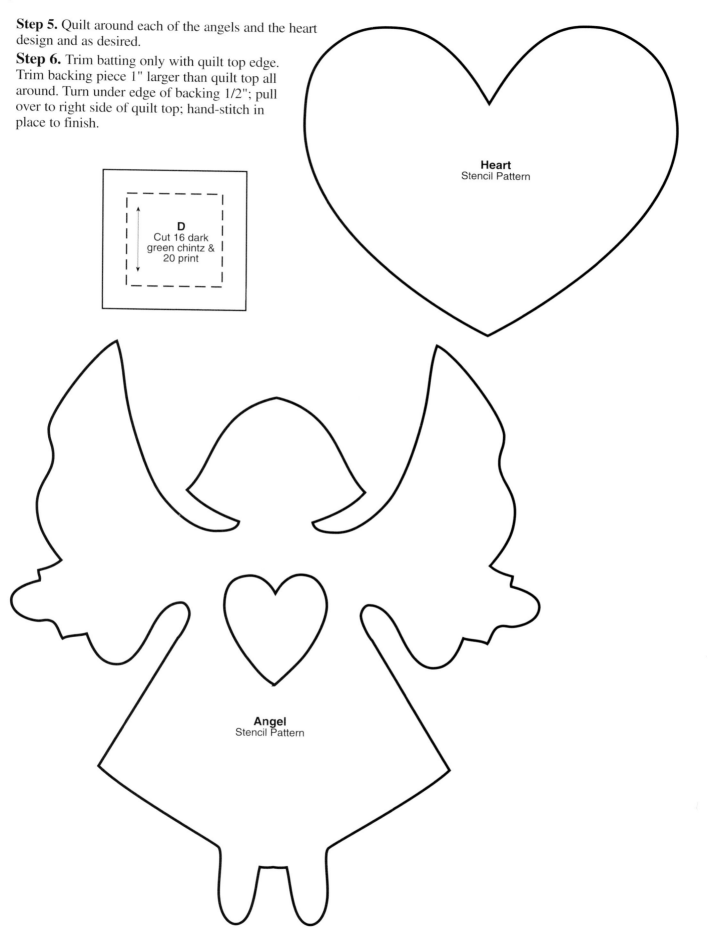

D
Cut 16 dark
green chintz &
20 print

Heart
Stencil Pattern

Angel
Stencil Pattern

GINGERBREAD TREES

By Angie Wilhite

Whip up this tiny wall hanging while baking gingerbread men cookies with your children!

Simple machine appliqué is used to create this tiny wall hanging, which can be made in a couple of hours, including the time needed for hand quilting.

Project Specifications
Skill Level: Easy
Quilt Size: 9" x 9"

Materials
- 9" x 9" piece green check fabric
- 11" x 11" backing piece
- 8" x 8" green solid or print for trees
- Black-and-beige check remnants
- 1/8 yard binding fabric
- 1 spool all-purpose thread to match fabric and ribbons
- 1 spool transparent nylon monofilament
- 1 spool hand-quilting thread
- 1/4 yard fusible transfer web
- 9" x 9" fabric stabilizer
- 11" x 11" quilter's fleece
- 19" of 7/8"-wide emerald single-face satin ribbon
- 2 (1/2") cabone rings
- 5 gingerbread boy buttons
- Jewel glue

Instructions
Step 1. Prewash all fabrics.

Step 2. Following manufacturer's instructions, apply fusible transfer web to backside of tree fabrics. Trace trees and trunks on paper side of fabrics. Cut out patterns; remove paper backing.

Step 3. Cut 7/8" x 19" fusible transfer webbing. Lay webbing on backside of emerald ribbon; fuse in place. Remove paper backing.

Step 4. Cut ribbon in two 9 1/2" pieces. Lay one 9 1/2" piece of ribbon horizontally across the middle of the quilt; fuse in place. Lay the second piece of ribbon ver-

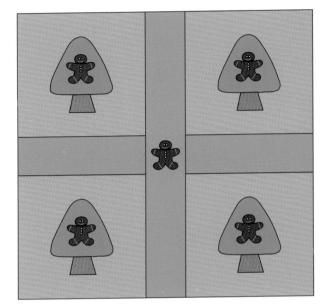

Gingerbread Trees
Placement Diagram
9" x 9"

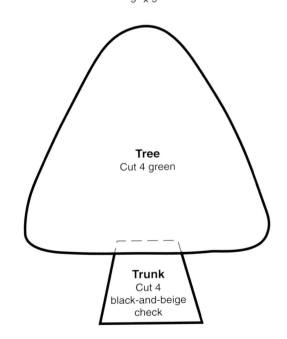

Tree
Cut 4 green

Trunk
Cut 4
black-and-beige
check

tically down the center of the quilt; fuse in place. Trim ribbon ends.

Step 5. Position a tree and trunk in each square; fuse in place.

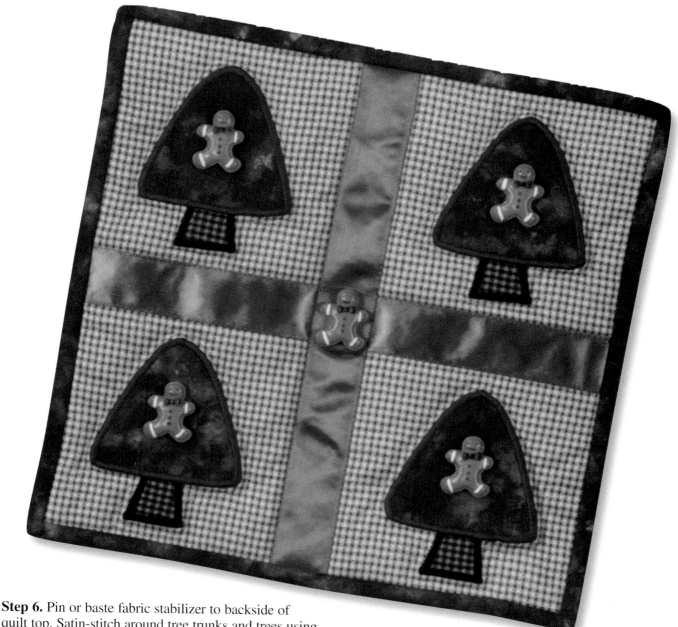

Step 6. Pin or baste fabric stabilizer to backside of quilt top. Satin-stitch around tree trunks and trees using matching all-purpose thread. Remove fabric stabilizer from the back of the design; trim threads.

Step 7. Place backing piece right side down on a flat surface. Lay batting on top of the backing piece; place top section right side up. Baste the layers together.

Step 8. Machine-stitch over horizontal ribbon through all three layers using transparent nylon thread; repeat procedure for vertical ribbon.

Step 9. Hand-quilt around tree shapes.

Step 10. Trim backing and batting even with edges of quilt top, if necessary.

Step 11. Cut 2" binding strip long enough to go around outside of quilt. Fold binding strip in half wrong sides together to make a long narrow strip; press.

Step 12. With raw edges even, lay binding on right side of quilt (do not start in a corner). Begin stitching 2" from the end of the binding strip; leave this 2" tail. Stitch, using a 1/4" seam, all around edges. When you get near the beginning end, fold tail under 1/4". Lay the other binding end inside this tail; finish sewing.

Step 13. Turn binding to the backside; blind-stitch in place to finish.

Step 14. Sew two 1/2" cabone rings to each top corner on the backside of the quilt to finish.

Step 15. Remove shanks from buttons. Use jewel glue to glue the gingerbread buttons to the center of each tree and to the center of vertical ribbon to finish.

STAR SNOWMAN

By Angie Wilhite

Working with felt to create quilted items is new to many of us. Look for plush, not thin, felt to create extra loft on the finished project.

If you like quick and easy projects, try machine- or hand-appliqué stitching on felt. The edges won't ravel, so they don't need to be turned under. If this type of project is new to you, you are in for a treat.

Project Specifications
Skill Level: Easy
Block Size: 4" x 4"
Quilt Size: 13" x 13"

Materials
- 1/2 yard red, 1/3 yard pirate green and 8" x 8" antique white Rainbow Classic Felt by Kunin Felt
- 1/6 yard binding felt
- 15" x 15" backing fabric
- 1/3 yard fusible transfer web
- 1 skein black embroidery floss
- 1 spool each black and beige all-purpose thread
- 1 spool white hand-quilting thread
- 1/2 yard quilter's fleece
- 20" of 1/8" black double-face satin ribbon
- 2 (1/2") cabone rings

Instructions
Step 1. Cut the following: four blocks green felt 4 1/2" x 4 1/2"; one piece red felt 8" x 8"; and two strips each red felt 2" x 4 1/2" and 2" x 13" and three strips 2" x 10".

Step 2. Following manufacturer's instructions, apply fusible transfer webbing to the backside of the 8" x 8" piece of red felt and the piece of white felt.

Step 3. Trace the snowman pattern on paper side of antique white felt; cut out pieces as directed. Remove paper backing. Repeat with star pattern on red felt.

Step 4. Lay a star on the center of each green block; fuse in place. Lay a snowman on the center of each star; fuse in place.

Step 5. Using 3 strands of black embroidery floss,

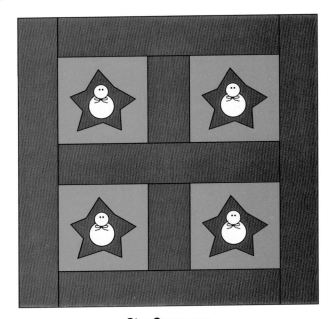

Star Snowman
Placement Diagram
13" x 13"

Star
Cut 4 red felt

Snowman
Cut 4 each white felt

blanket-stitch around the edges of stars and snowmen. Using 2 strands of black embroidery floss, make two French knots for eyes. Using 2 strands of black embroidery floss, make two X's on each snowman referring to the pattern for placement.

Step 6. Cut 1/8" black ribbon into four 5" lengths; tie

four bows and trim ends. Tack a bow to each snow-man neck.

Step 7. Join two 4 1/2" blocks with a 2" x 4 1/2" red strip; press seams toward blocks. Repeat for second row. Join the two rows with a 2" x 10" red strip; sew the remaining 2" x 10" strips to the top and bottom. Press seams toward strips.

Step 8. Sew a 2" x 13" strip to each side; press seams toward strips.

Step 9. Place backing piece right side down on a flat surface. Lay batting on top of the backing piece; place top section right side up. Baste the layers together.

Step 10. Hand-quilt 1/4" from all seams. Quilt around star and snowman shapes, if desired.

Step 11. Trim backing and batting even with edges of quilt top, if necessary.

Step 12. Cut 1 1/2" felt binding strip long enough to go around outside of quilt; piece several strips together, if necessary.

Step 13. With raw edges even, lay binding on quilt (do not start in a corner). Stitch, using a 1/4" seam, all around edges. When you get near the beginning end, lay binding inside the sewn binding and finish sewing in place.

Step 14. Turn binding to the backside; blind-stitch in place to finish.

Step 15. Sew two 1/2" cabone rings to each top cor-ner on the backside of the quilt to finish.

POINSETTIA QUILT

Continued from page 119

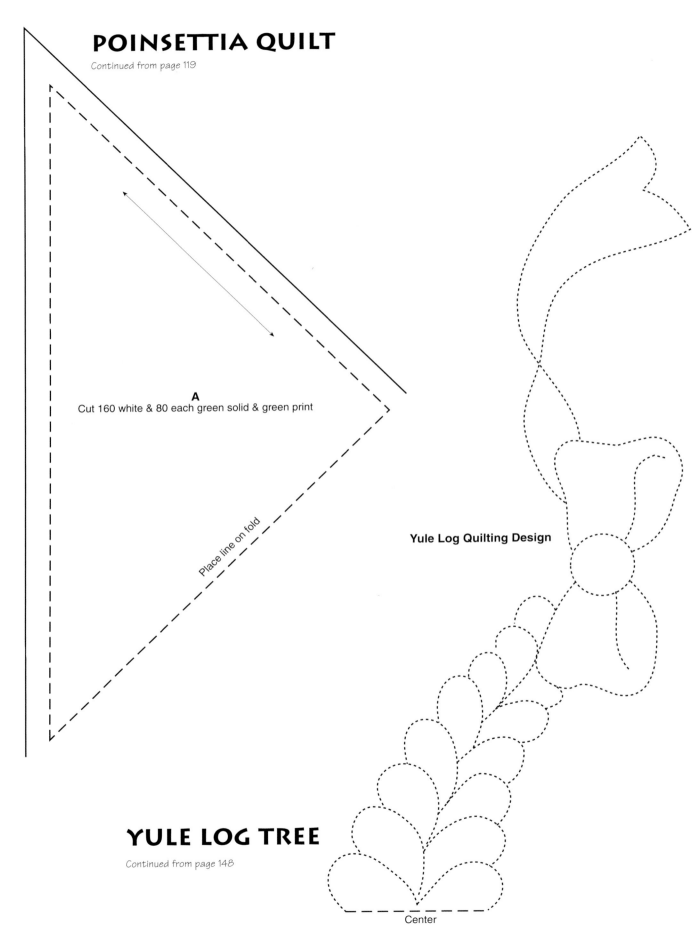

A
Cut 160 white & 80 each green solid & green print

Place line on fold

Yule Log Quilting Design

YULE LOG TREE

Continued from page 148

Center

SANTA ON THE MOON SWEATSHIRT

Continued from page 31

Bag
Cut 1 black check

Heart
Cut 1 burgundy print

ACKNOWLEDGMENTS

We would like to thank the following manufacturers who have provided our quilting designers with materials and supplies. We appreciate their contribution to the production of this book.

Kunin Felt Co.
• Rainbow Classic Felt
Used in *Yo-Yo Ornaments* and *Star Snowman*

Pellon
• Wonder-Under Transfer Web, Sof-Shape, Fusible Fleece and Stitch-n-Tear
Used in the following projects: *Santa Vest, Sledding Santa Sweatshirt, Santa on the Moon Sweatshirt, Tree Santa Sweatshirt, Folk Tie Santa Tote Bag, Santa Place Mat,* *Napkin & Bread Cover, Christmas Tree Place Mat and Napkin, Santa & Bag Place Mat & Napkin, Christmas Tea Towel, Gingerbread Trees, Star Snowman* and *Homespun Holidays* table runner, place mat, napkin, tea cozy and apron

VIP Fabrics
• Homespun Holidays Collection, Cotton Candy Solids Collection and Starry Nights Collection
Used in *Homespun Holidays* table runner, place mat, napkin, tea cozy and apron

Angels All Around

5 Delightful Angel Projects
Bring Joy to Your Home

Designs by Jodi Warren

Edited by Sandra L. Hatch

HOUSE of
WHITE
BIRCHES

PUBLISHERS
SINCE 1947

Hark! The Herald Angels Tree Skirt & Stocking

Christmas carols are some of our favorite songs. The theme of Hark! The Herald Angels Sing *is the basis for this inspiring tree skirt and matching stocking.*

Project Specifications

Tree Skirt Size: Approximately 45" in diameter
Stocking Size: Approximately 8" x 17"

Fabric & Batting

- 1 5/8 yards red print for background
- 3/8 yard bright goldenrod (center star, dress hem, halo and flower)
- 1/2 yard medium bright green stripe (skirt heart and flower heart, checkerboard, piping and binding)
- 1/4 yard each cream-with-white check (banner background) and white-with-white check (clouds)
- 1/6 yard deep goldenrod (center star edge)
- 1/8 yard each light green (checkerboard, stocking square bands), bright blue (banner borders, dress, flower and stocking toe and cuff), medium dark blue stripe (sleeves, petals and circle and banner and stocking bands), white-on-white print (wings) and muslin with white stripe (apron)
- Scraps black (hair), skin tone (face and hands), fuchsia (flower), red mottled (smaller hearts and flower) and dark green (leaves)
- 48" x 48" square thin batting for skirt; 20" x 20" square for stocking
- 1 3/4 yards backing fabric for skirt; 20" x 20" square for stocking

Supplies

- 1 yard fabric stabilizer
- 1 1/2 yards light or medium-weight fusible transfer web
- 1 1/4 yards 3/16" narrow poly cording for stocking piping
- 3 red 1 1/8" red heart buttons for stocking
- Black and cream acrylic tole paint (eye details)

Stitch-n-Tear from Pellon, HeatnBond fusible transfer web and JHB International #24961 buttons used on Tree Skirt and Stocking.

ANGELS ALL AROUND is published by House of White Birches, 306 East Parr Road, Berne, IN 46711. Printed in USA. Copyright © 1996 House of White Birches. Editor: Sandra L. Hatch; Associate Editor: Jeanne Stauffer; Technical Artist: Connie Rand; Production: Scott Runkel; Photography: Tammy Christian, Nora Elsesser; Cover Design: Shaun Venish; Product Marketing: Claudia Claussen.
RETAILERS: If you would like to carry this pattern book or any other House of White Birches publication, call The Needlecraft Shop at (903) 636–4011 to set up an account.
ADDITIONAL PUBLICATIONS: Write today for a complete listing of publications available from House of White Birches. Send to: Publications Listing, 306 East Parr Road, Berne, IN 46711.
Every effort has been made to ensure that the instructions in this pattern book are complete and accurate. We cannot, however, take responsibility for human error, typographical mistakes or variations in individual work.

- Rose acrylic stencil paint or rose blusher (cheek coloring)
- All-purpose thread to closely match appliqué fabrics
- 1 spool contrasting color quilting thread

Basic Paper-Piecing Instructions

Using paper-piecing foundations makes accurate stitching possible. It uses a photocopy of the piecing diagram as a foundation guide for positioning and sewing the design component patches. Note that since these will be seen from the backside of the construction, they may appear in mirror image from the finished project. The following is a list of pointers for this fun and accurate method.

1. Trim photocopied diagrams leaving roughly 1/2" space beyond outlines, which are the final cutting lines. Instead of preparing templates and cutting shapes, cut fabric strips of designated widths and convenient lengths.

2. Identify areas #1 and #2 and their assigned fabrics; layer one strip of each right sides together, straight edges aligned. Position this strip pair against the unprinted side of the foundation diagram with fabric #1 next to paper, directly beneath and covering the #1 area. The diagram seam line shared by #1 and #2 should be 1/4" in from aligned raw edges. (Raising paper off the working surface to allow some light to penetrate may assist with alignment.)

3. Shorten machine stitching to 16–18 stitches per inch. Stitch on designated line (begin and end two stitches beyond actual ends of line). Turn foundation over, press #2 piece away from #1 piece. Trim excess strips roughly 1/4" larger than the area they are intended to cover; trim excess from seam allowance beyond stitching to scant 1/4".

4. Position fabric #3 strip against patch #2 (right sides together), extending edge at least 1/4" past seam line shared by #2 and #3. Stitch, trim and press as above. Continue adding strips in order until section is completed.

5. Place rotary ruler along section outer solid line; trim away excess fabric and paper. Set section aside until all

sections are completed to help stabilize bias-grained sections.

6. To remove paper, fold along stitching line of area added last; tear away at perforations made by stitching. Continue removing in reverse order until all paper is detached. Gentle handling will minimize stretching.

7. To avoid tearing foundation paper prematurely when unpicking is necessary, use a seam ripper or sharp-pointed scissors to clip the stitching before removing and replacing strip.

8. Odd-shaped patches may make it difficult to align fabric strips so that when stitched and pressed open the required design area will be covered. To assist in positioning, fold the paper foundation (with attached fabrics) inward along the seam line to be stitched (print sides folded together). The shape can now be seen (looking through the foundation) just as the finished fabric patch will appear. Position over right side of fabric strip so area in question is covered. Unfold paper and proceed as usual. When stitched and pressed back in place, fabric will cover the area just as when the paper was folded. (See Figure 6).

Project Instructions

Note: Strip cutting measurements include a 1/4" seam allowance. Patchwork template diagrams show seam lines as dashed lines and cutting lines as solid lines. Appliqué templates are given finished size; add a seam allowance when cutting for hand-appliqué.

Tree Skirt

Preparing for Paper Piecing

1. Photocopy paper-piecing patterns given to use as stitching foundations as follows: six Angel blocks; six

Angel Tree Skirt
Placement Diagram
Approximately 45" Diameter

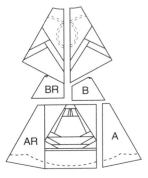

Figure 1
Assemble Angel and Star sections as shown.

Right Center Stars; six Left Center Stars; and eight Banner blocks. Trim excess 1/2" beyond outer solid lines. *Note: Half-banner panels will face each other across center back opening so only a right and left half need to be completed. For half-blocks, trim one photocopy 1/4" to the left of the center line and another 1/4" to the right of the center line.*

2. Cut strips across the width of the fabric in the designated sizes for paper-piecing as follows (begin with one or two strips; cut more as needed): skin tone—1"; bright goldenrod—1", 3" and 4 1/4"; deep goldenrod—1 1/4"; bright blue—1 1/2" and 2 3/4"; red background—5" and 2 3/4"; muslin stripe—3 1/2"; cream check—6 1/2"; and dark blue—1".

Angel Blocks & Star Sections

1. Review Basic Paper-Piecing Instructions, then complete six Angel blocks, adding patches in order with indicated fabrics. Use previously cut strips combined with scraps to complete blocks.

2. Transfer dashed skirt curve guideline to fabric section 19. Transfer position of large dots to the wrong side of the fabric of each block. Trim paper and block on outer solid lines; remove paper from sections.

3. Complete six Right and six Left Center Star sections with paper-piecing. Trim paper and block on outer solid line. Transfer position of large dots to the wrong side of the fabric of each section; remove paper from sections.

4. Trace and cut 12 of each A and B (reverse half of each); transfer shaded skirt curve guideline and large dots to fabrics.

5. Join A's and ARs to sides of Angel blocks referring to Figure 1 and aligning dots with crossing seams at block edges; press seams toward A's.

6. Position B's and BRs referring to Figure 1, aligning large dots. Sew to end of seam line on B pieces (seam will be completed later); press seam toward B's.

Blossom Banner Blocks

1. For checkerboard sections, cut seven strips each 1" x 11 1/2" from bright green stripe and light green. Stitch long edges of opposite-fabric strip pairs; press seams toward bright green.

2. Cut each strip unit into 1" units. Rotate alternate units to line up opposite colors. Join in five 11-unit sections and two seven-unit sections as shown in Figure 2; press seams toward one end of section.

3. Complete one left-half, one right-half and five whole

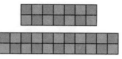

Figure 2
Join 7 units to make 1 section.
Join 11 units to make 1 section.

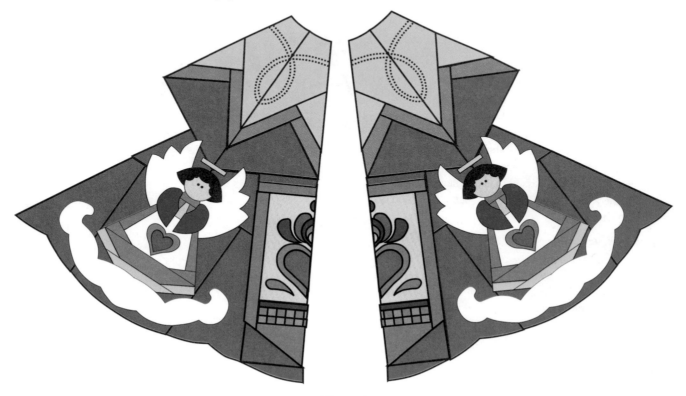

Figure 3
Join Blossom Banner sections with the Star-Angel section.

Blossom Banner blocks with paper-piecing foundations. Begin by centering checkerboard section behind area #1 (dark green end squares toward top) with long seam line aligned on Placement guideline; pin or baste in place.

4. Complete Blossom Banner blocks. Transfer dashed skirt curve guideline to fabric section 9. Trim paper and blocks on outer solid lines; remove paper from sections.

5. Cut seven bright blue C strips 1 1/4" x 7 1/2" and seven red background D strips 1" x 7 1/2". Sew C, then D to top edge of each Blossom Banner block (refer to drawing, page 8); press seams toward C. Trim excess strips even with half-block edges.

Angel & Blossom Appliqué

Note: Directions are given for machine appliqué. If preferred, complete appliqué using hand-appliqué methods by cutting patches with seam allowances added, and turning exposed edges under to blind-stitch in place.

1. Prepare appliqué templates from Angel Appliqué, Banner block hearts and flowers and Cloud patterns. Trace templates, reversing as needed, onto paper side of fusible transfer webbing.

2. Roughly trim shapes around outer edge; trim excess within all but smallest shapes, leaving approximately 1/4" fusing margin. Use hot iron to fuse shapes to wrong side of appropriate fabrics. Carefully cut out on traced lines; remove paper backing.

3. Arrange prepared shapes over Angel and Banner blocks according to full-size drawings with face under hair, larger blossom and heart shapes under smaller similar shapes, cloud below hem seam, etc. Press with iron to fuse in place.

4. Cut sections of fabric stabilizer larger than appliqué area. Pin or baste in place against the wrong side of blocks directly under appliqué area.

5. Using closely matching thread in upper and bobbin feeds with a medium-wide machine zigzag stitch, overcast all exposed appliqué areas. *Note: Try to complete stitching in best order so that previously stitched ends can be caught in subsequent stitching. When this is not possible, lock stitching at beginning and end by stitching two or three times in place and pulling thread ends to underside of work. Practice manipulating appliqué work so stitching is uniform with smooth curves and consistent straight lines.*

6. When appliqué is complete, remove basting; tear away fabric stabilizer and foundation sheet along stitching lines around and within all appliqués.

Joining Skirt Sections

1. Join six Angel/Center Star sections side by side along Star edge. Insert Banner half-blocks into appropriate space at each end of assembly as shown in Figure 3.

Stitch side edge to A-B edges, aligning large dots to crossing seam; press seams toward Banner blocks.

2. Insert whole Banner blocks into remaining spaces; stitch side edges. Align Banner upper edges with Center Star section lower edges; complete stitching between marks (overlap stitching at each end to ensure strong seam); press seams toward Banner blocks.

Finishing

1. Use the rounded end of a fine tole brush to make black pin-dot eyes and cream centers. Use stencil brush with lightly loaded stencil paint to brush on cheek color (or use makeup blusher).

2. Transfer loop quilting design lines to Center Star sections using a water-erasable marker or pencil. Mark the arch lines between Angel and Banner blocks (extend lines) to echo-quilting lines at Banner block sides. Also mark quilting lines 1/4" inside lower seams of bright goldenrod sections of large and small Center Star points, 1/4" echo line around Banner block and appliqué silhouette, and 1" echo line below Center Star points in B.

3. Prepare backing piece 48" x 48".

4. Sandwich batting between the prepared backing piece and the finished tree skirt top. Straighten, pin, then baste all outer curve and center back edges within seam allowance; baste layers together.

5. Quilt on all marked lines as well as next to checkerboard lines, around appliqué shapes and color-block patchwork sections. *Note: Stiffness created by fusing and machine-appliqué may make quilting more difficult.* When quilting is complete, trim excess batting and backing fabric even with skirt raw edges all around.

6. Cut enough lengths of scant 1 1/2"-wide bias strips from medium bright green stripe to make 7 yards of binding. Sew short pieces together to make one long strip.

7. To prepare 3/8" double-fold binding, lay a 3/4" strip of manila-folder-weight paper down center wrong side of bias, pressing both raw edges over paper. Slide paper along to complete single-fold press of entire length. Align creased edges right side out and press for double-fold bias tape.

8. Cut two 8" lengths for ties; fold one end under; stitch folded ends together. Baste raw edges of ties in place at each center back edge (ties lying toward skirt) approximately 7" below upper edge.

9. Cut a 30" length for center circle opening; set aside. Beginning at top center back edge, open folded binding and lay outer fold line over the 1/4" edge seam line on right side of skirt, binding flat and inward; stitch along crease line through all layers, mitering corners. End at left top center back edge; trim ends even with center circle opening edge.

10. Fold binding to skirt backside, enclosing raw edges. Align over previous stitching and blind-stitch in place to finish.

Angel Stocking
Placement Diagram
Approximately 8" x 17"

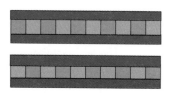

Figure 4
Make 2 units as shown.

11. Measure in approximately 7 1/2" from 30" binding length; attach binding to center opening at that point, stretching around center circle as stitching proceeds. Measure 7 1/2" of remaining binding length past circle opening; trim excess. Fold 1/4" under at ends; stitch extended edges of tie lengths together. Fold binding on circle opening to backside; blind-stitch in place over previous stitching.

Angel Stocking

1. Photocopy one Angel block paper-piecing diagram; trim excess leaving 1/2" beyond outer solid lines, including solid line below hem section noted as stocking cutting line.

2. Cut fabric strips (skin tone, bright blue, muslin stripe, bright goldenrod and red background only) for paper foundation work as in step 2 for tree skirt. Complete one block as directed for Angel block, cutting section 19 shorter as indicated by line on pattern. Trim paper and block on outer solid lines; remove paper sections.

3. Cut the following: two strips 2 1/4" x 6 1/4" red background for strip E; one strip red background 3 3/4" x 9" for strip F; one strip red background 1 1/8" x 9 1/4" for strip G; four strips medium dark blue stripe 7/8" x 9" for H strips; one strip each bright blue 2 3/4" x 9" (for piece I cuff) and 2 1/2" x 7 1/4" (for piece J toe); two strips medium bright green stripe 1 1/4" x 15 1/2" for strip K; and two strips light green 1 1/4" x 15 1/2" for strip L.

4. Referring to Stocking pattern for placement, stitch one E strip to each side edge of Angel block; stitch an F strip to upper edge of block and G to lower edge; press seams toward the blocks.

5. Stitch K to each L along long edges; press seams toward K. Cut strips into 1 1/4" units. Join units as shown in Figure 4; press seams toward medium bright green.

6. Join H strips to each long edge of both K-L sections; press seams toward H. Center each K-L-H section along upper and lower edge of pieced section; press seams toward H. Sew the I strip to upper assembly edge and strip J to lower edge; press seams toward H.

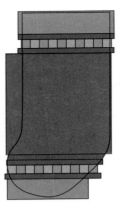

Figure 5
Stitch pieces together
as shown to make
stocking base. Transfer
stocking pattern; cut
out shapes.

7. Complete Angel block machine appliqué as for tree skirt. Referring to Figure 5, transfer stocking outline to stitched section. Transfer arch quilting lines to each side of Angel appliqué, squares on cuff and 1/2" vertical lines on toe strip.

8. Divide stocking batting into two 10" x 20" sections; cut two matching lining and one red background stocking back sections.

9. Layer one lining piece with batting and stocking front. Quilt on marked lines by hand or machine. Layer stocking back, batting and lining sections; machine- or hand-quilt 1" grid lines.

10. Cut 1"-wide bias strips from medium bright green stripe; join together to form a 1 1/4-yard length. Enclose cording next to wrong side of bias strip; machine-baste through two fabric layers close to cord thickness (use zipper foot); trim excess seam allowance past stitching to 1/4".

11. With piping pointing inward, position and baste stitching exactly over stocking outline. Taper piping into seam allowance at top opening seam line.

12. Lay stocking front over quilted back, linings out; stitch around following previous basting on outline; lock stitches at opening edges.

13. Trim away excess to 1/4"; trim top edges even and overcast raw seam edges. Turn right side out.

14. Prepare a 20" length of 3/8" double-fold bias binding using bright blue as directed in step 7 in the Finishing section for tree skirt. From this, cut a 4 1/2" piece for loop; stitch folded edges together.

15. Place loop ends together; machine-baste over seam at upper right side of stocking opening, loop facing downward. Apply binding to opening edge, beginning at center back. Fold one end under and overlap other end when they meet.

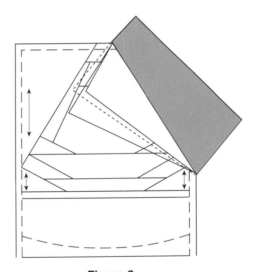

Figure 6
To check fabric alignment on foundation papers, fold the paper back along the seam line to see the shape as it will appear.

Drawing shows complete Blossom Banner block.

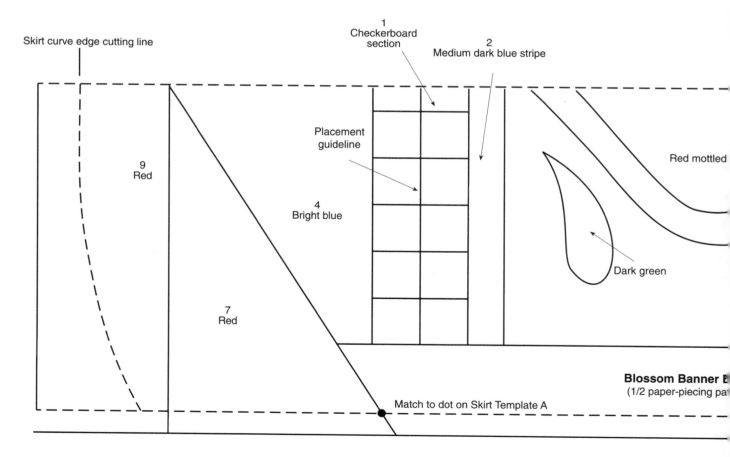

Skirt curve edge cutting line

1
Checkerboard
section

2
Medium dark blue stripe

Placement
guideline

Red mottled

9
Red

4
Bright blue

Dark green

7
Red

Match to dot on Skirt Template A

Blossom Banner B
(1/2 paper-piecing pat

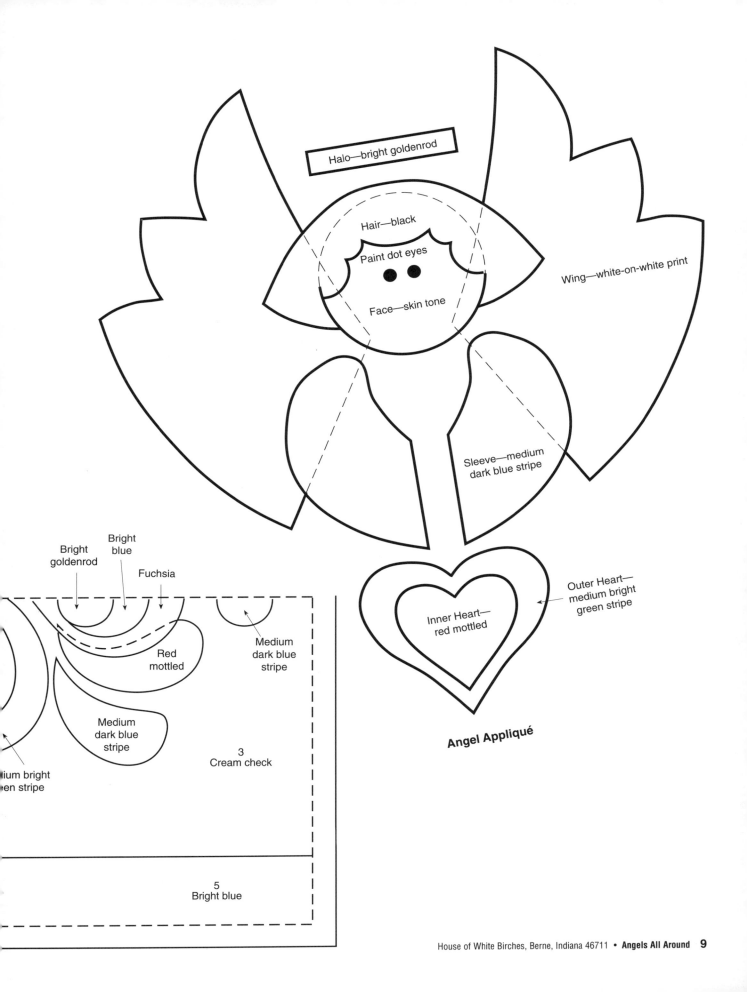

Halo—bright goldenrod

Hair—black

Paint dot eyes

Face—skin tone

Wing—white-on-white print

Sleeve—medium dark blue stripe

Bright goldenrod

Bright blue

Fuchsia

Medium dark blue stripe

Red mottled

Medium dark blue stripe

3
Cream check

Outer Heart—medium bright green stripe

Inner Heart—red mottled

ium bright
en stripe

5
Bright blue

Angel Appliqué

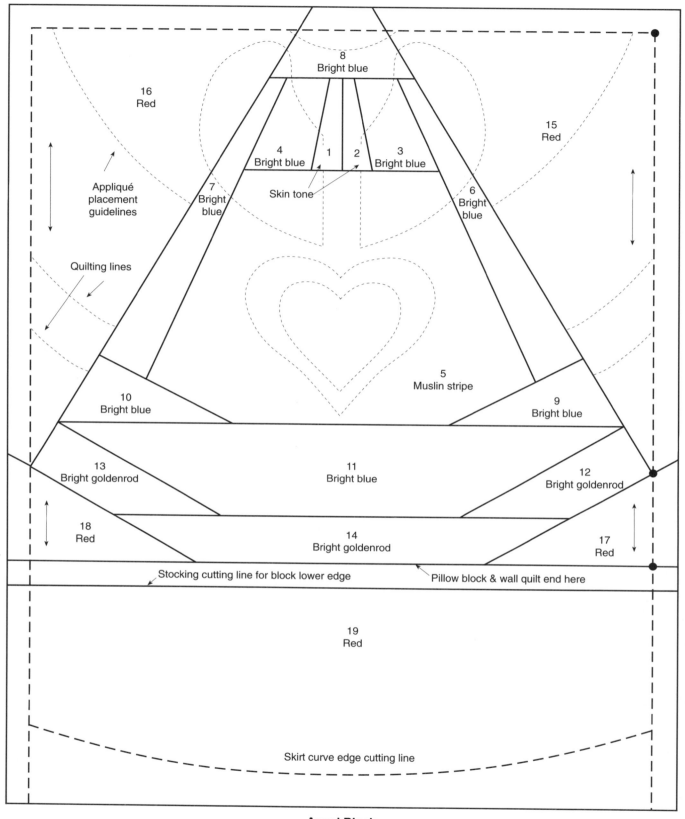

Angel Block
(Full-size paper-piecing pattern)

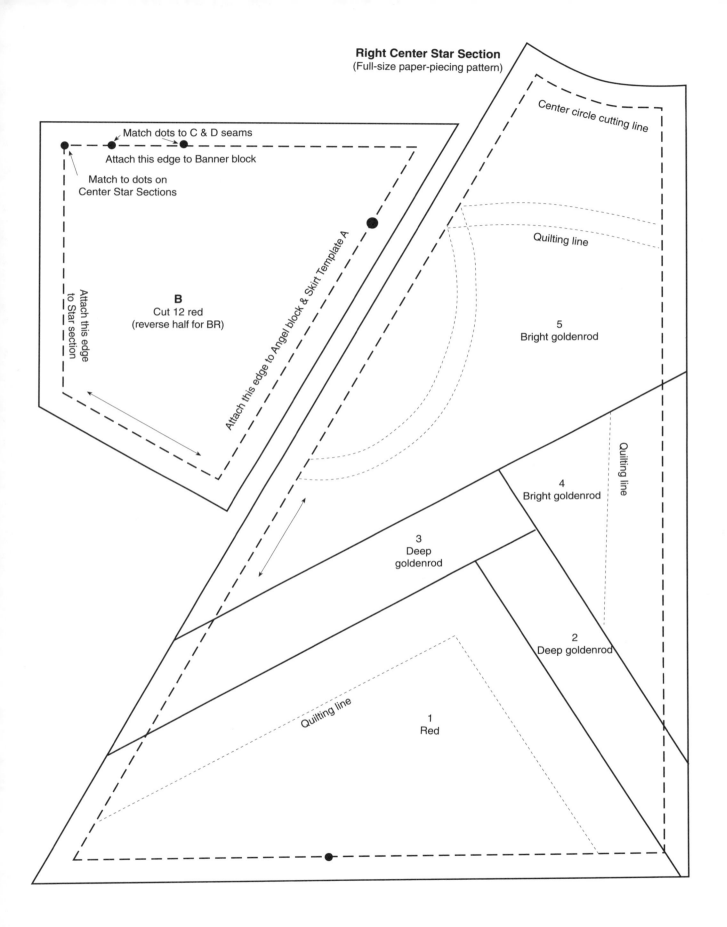

Right Center Star Section
(Full-size paper-piecing pattern)

Center circle cutting line

Quilting line

Match dots to C & D seams

Attach this edge to Banner block

Match to dots on
Center Star Sections

Attach this edge to Angel block & Skirt Template A

Attach this edge
to Star section

B
Cut 12 red
(reverse half for BR)

5
Bright goldenrod

Quilting line

4
Bright goldenrod

3
Deep
goldenrod

2
Deep goldenrod

Quilting line

1
Red

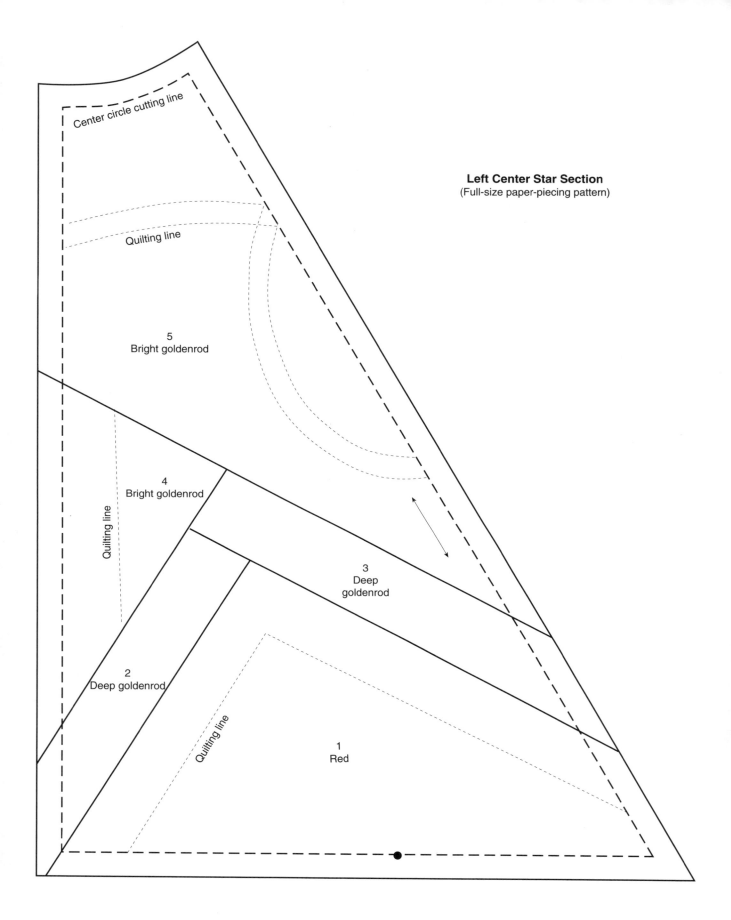

Left Center Star Section
(Full-size paper-piecing pattern)

Center circle cutting line

Quilting line

5
Bright goldenrod

Quilting line

4
Bright goldenrod

3
Deep
goldenrod

2
Deep goldenrod

Quilting line

1
Red

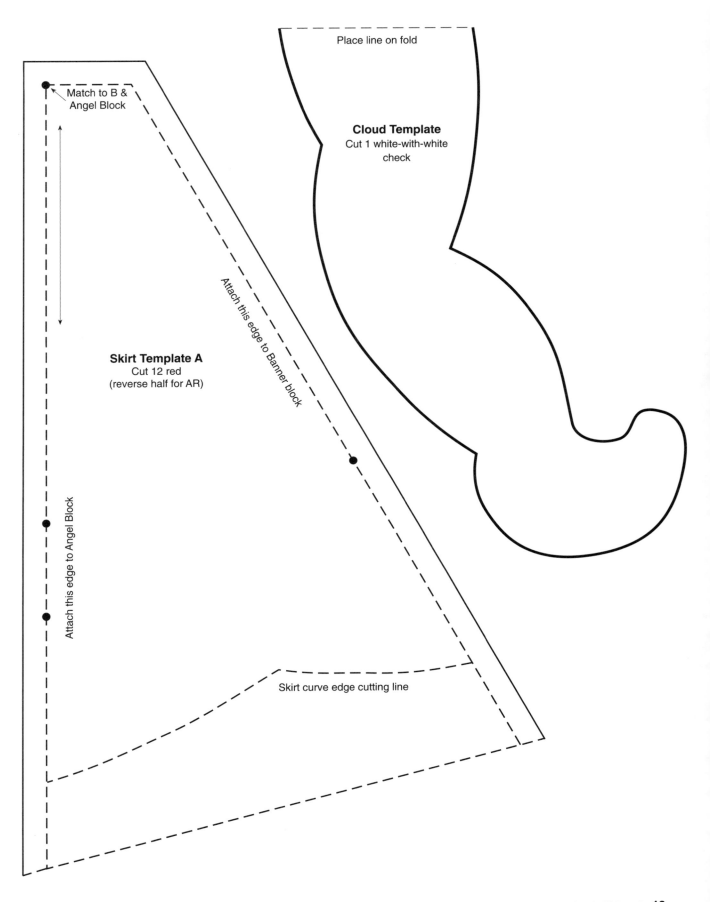

Place line on fold

Cloud Template
Cut 1 white-with-white
check

Match to B &
Angel Block

Skirt Template A
Cut 12 red
(reverse half for AR)

Attach this edge to Banner block

Attach this edge to Angel Block

Skirt curve edge cutting line

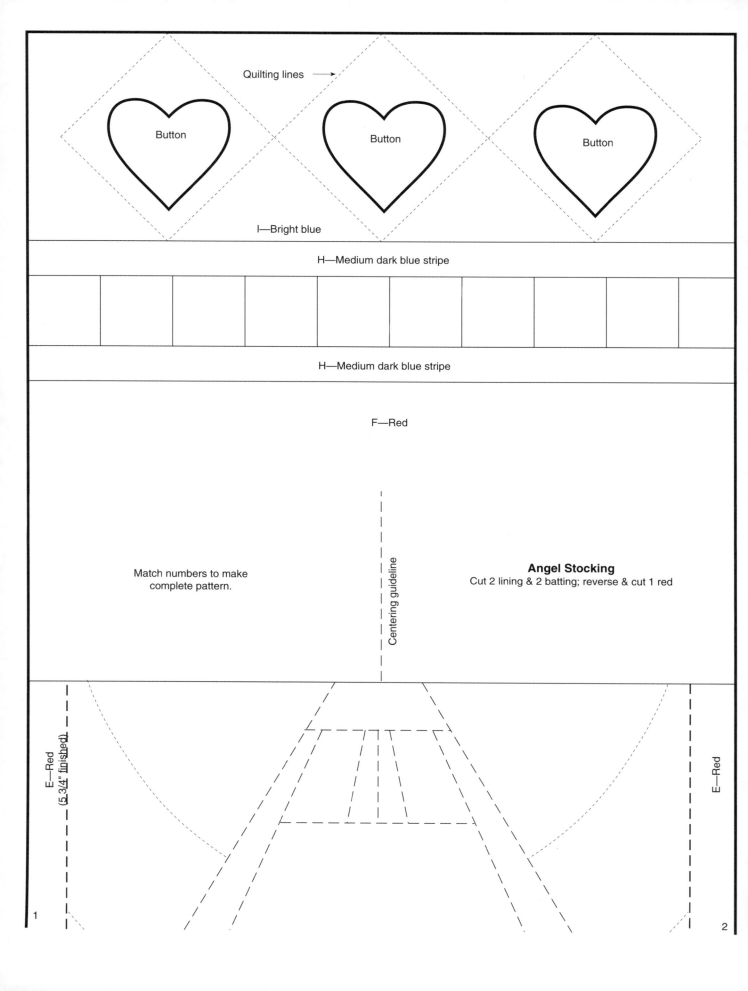

Quilting lines →

Button

Button

Button

I—Bright blue

H—Medium dark blue stripe

H—Medium dark blue stripe

F—Red

Match numbers to make
complete pattern.

Centering guideline

Angel Stocking
Cut 2 lining & 2 batting; reverse & cut 1 red

E—Red
(5 3/4" finished)

E—Red

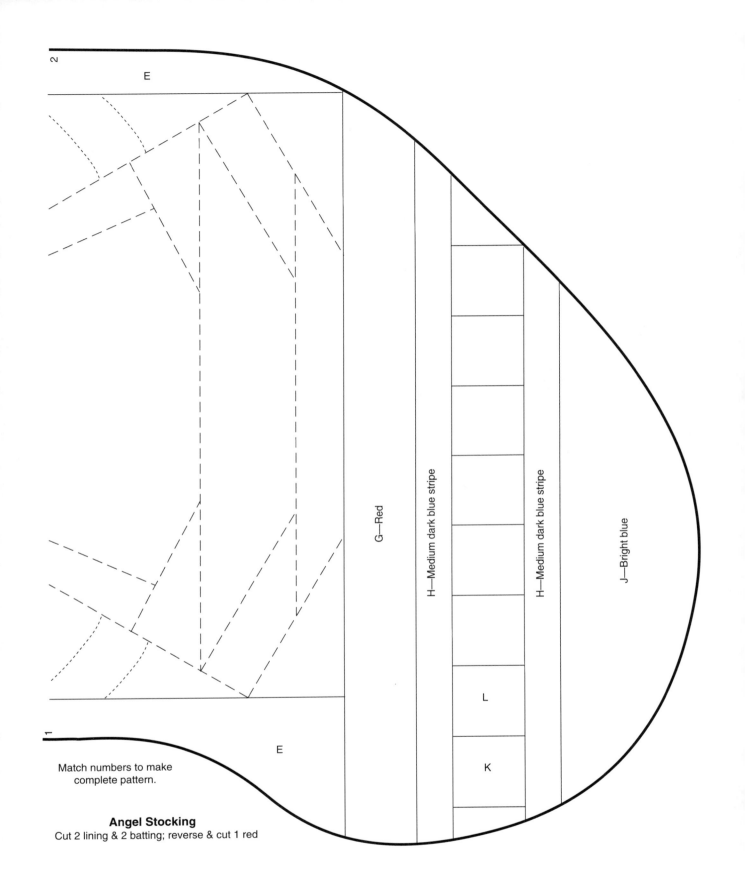

2

E

G—Red

H—Medium dark blue stripe

H—Medium dark blue stripe

J—Bright blue

L

K

1

Match numbers to make
complete pattern.

Angel Stocking
Cut 2 lining & 2 batting; reverse & cut 1 red

E

Angel & Penn Dutch Decorator Pillows

Use darker and more subdued Christmas colors to create these pretty pillows. The angel design is used on one and the heart design used on the tree skirt is used on the other one. These pillows would look good in any room any time of the year.

Angel Block Pillow
Placement Diagram
16" x 20"

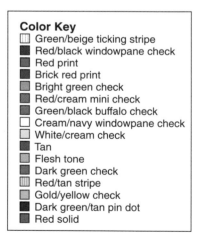

Color Key
- ▥ Green/beige ticking stripe
- ■ Red/black windowpane check
- ■ Red print
- ■ Brick red print
- ▨ Bright green check
- ■ Red/cream mini check
- ■ Green/black buffalo check
- □ Cream/navy windowpane check
- ▨ White/cream check
- ■ Tan
- ▨ Flesh tone
- ■ Dark green check
- ▥ Red/tan stripe
- ▨ Gold/yellow check
- ■ Dark green/tan pin dot
- ■ Red solid

Project Specifications

Pillow Size: 16" x 20" for 16" pillow form

Fabric & Batting

- 1/4 yard green/beige ticking stripe for background
- 3/8 yard each red/black windowpane check (Angel button bands) and red print (Penn Dutch button bands)
- 1/8 yard each brick red print (dress, large heart, block sashing), bright green check (large apron heart, checkerboard, corner squares), and red/cream mini check (sashing)
- 1 yard green/black buffalo check (backing, sashing)
- Scraps cream/navy windowpane check (apron), white/cream check (checkerboard, wings), tan (hair, flower), flesh tone (face, hands), dark green check (hem, sleeves, small flower heart), red/tan stripe (small apron heart), gold/yellow check (halo, flower), dark green/tan pin dot (flower, teardrops), and red solid (flower dots)
- 1/2 yard thin batiste or voile
- 1/2 yard muslin
- 2 pieces thin batting 18" x 18"

Supplies

- 1/8 yard each fabric stabilizer and lightweight fusible transfer web
- 16 bright green 1 1/8" buttons
- 1 spool each all-purpose threads to match fabrics
- 1 spool contrasting quilting thread
- Black and cream acrylic tole paint
- Rose acrylic stencil paint for makeup blusher
- Stencil brush
- 2 polyester 16" pillow forms

Angel Pillow

1. Complete one Angel block as directed in steps 1 and 2 on page 4, substituting fabrics referring to color photo on the cover.

2. Cut two strips green/beige ticking stripe 1 1/4" x 6 1/4" for M and one strip 3 3/4" x 8 1/2" for N. *Note: Try to match stripes in M and N with background stripes on paper-pieced section.*

3. Cut two strips red/cream mini check 2" x 8 1/2" for O and two strips 2" x 9 1/2" for P. Cut four squares

bright green check 2" x 2" for Q. Cut two strips green/black buffalo check 3" x 12 1/2" for R and two strips 2 1/2" x 16 1/2" for Y.

4. Cut one piece green/black buffalo check 16 1/2" x 16 1/2" for backing.

5. Cut two strips red pane check 6 1/2" x 32 1/2" for band Z.

6. Stitch M strip to side edges of Angel block. Stitch matching N to top edge. Refer to color photo. Prepare and arrange Angel block appliqué using pattern on page 9. Complete machine appliqué as for tree skirt on page 5.

7. Use the rounded end of a fine tole brush to make black pin-dot eyes. Dot center of eyes with cream paint. Use stencil brush with lightly loaded stencil paint for cheek color (or use makeup blusher).

8. Sew an O strip to the top and bottom of the appliquéd block; press. Sew a Q square to each end of the P strips; sew to remaining sides of center; press.

9. Sew R strips to opposite sides of center; press. Sew a Y strip to the top and bottom; press. Refer to Figure 1 for placement of strips.

10. Mark 1/4" echo quilting lines around appliqué shapes. Mark arch lines below wings as shown on Stocking pattern on page 14. Mark a line down the center of each O and P strip and a line 1" from the O-Y seams and the P-R seams.

11. Cut one piece voile or batiste 18" x 18". Sandwich a piece of batting between pillow top and one batiste or voile square. Pin or baste layers together for quilting. Quilt on all marked lines and in the ditch of all seams.

12. Cut one piece muslin 18" x 18". Baste to the green/black buffalo check pillow backing. Join the top edges of quilted pillow panel and back; overcast or serge raw edge of seam.

13. With wrong sides together, press a crease down the length of each Z band 2 1/4" from each edge. *Note: When finished, bands will be three layers thick.*

14. Unfold band; fold one edge of band under 1/4"; press. Stitch other edge right sides together along one long edge of pillow panel; press seams toward band. Repeat for second edge. Fold pillow panel with right sides together; pin raw edges together, including the Z bands, matching the band seam on each side; stitch.

15. Turn pillow right side out. Fold band along creases enclosing seam on inside edge; pin or baste in place. Working from the right side, topstitch next to seam through all band layers.

16. Referring to Figure 3, mark buttonhole positions on band front layers. Stitch buttonholes; slit open. Mark button positions centered below buttonholes on inside of band back layer and attach.

17. Insert pillow form; button closed to finish.

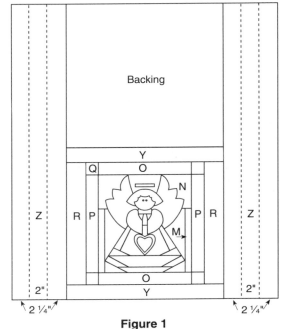

Figure 1
Sew strips to the Angel block panel as shown.

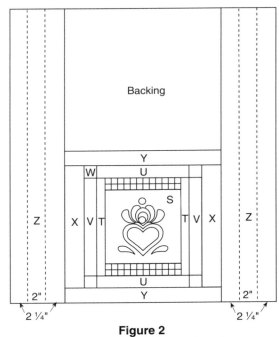

Figure 2
Sew strips to the Penn block panel as shown.

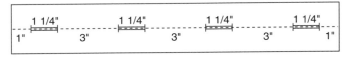

Figure 3
Mark buttonholes on bands as shown.

Penn Dutch Pillow
Placement Diagram
16" x 20"

Color Key
▨ Green/beige ticking stripe
■ Red/black windowpane check
■ Red print
■ Brick red print
■ Bright green check
■ Red/cream mini check
■ Green/black buffalo check
□ Cream/navy windowpane check
▨ White/cream check
■ Tan
■ Flesh tone
■ Dark green check
▦ Red/tan stripe
■ Gold/yellow check
■ Dark green/tan pin dot
■ Red solid

Penn Dutch Pillow

1. Cut one piece 6 1/2" x 7 1/2" green/beige ticking stripe for S background.

2. Cut two pieces 1 1/2" x 9 1/2" red/cream check for T. Cut two pieces 2" x 8 1/2" brick red print for U and two pieces 2" x 9 1/2" for V. Cut four squares bright green check 2" x 2" for W. Cut two strips 2 1/2" x 16 1/2" green/black buffalo check for Y and two strips 3" x 12 1/2" for X.

3. Cut one piece green/black buffalo check 16 1/2" x 16 1/2" for backing.

4. Cut two strips red print 6 1/4" x 32 1/2" for band Z.

5. Using Banner appliqué pattern on pages 9 and 10 and referring to color photo of Penn Dutch pillow for color of pieces, appliqué design on the S background piece.

6. Cut 1" x 13" checkerboard strips, two each from white/cream check and bright green plaid. Join strips; cut into 1" units. Assemble two 12-unit sections as in steps 1 and 2 for Banner blocks on page 4. Join the sections to the top and bottom of the S panel. Stitch T strips to sides; press seams toward strips.

7. Sew a U strip to the top and bottom of the appliquéd panel; press seams toward strips. Sew a W square to each end of the V strips; sew to sides; press seams toward V. Sew an X strip to two long sides; press. Sew a Y strip to the top and bottom; press.

8. Mark 1/4" echo quilting lines around appliqué shapes. Mark a line down the center of each U and V strip and a line 1" from the U-Y seams and the V-X seams.

9. Finish as for Angel pillow steps 11–17.

Angel Wall Quilt

This loving angel takes on a very different look in this wall quilt. Use fabrics to match the tree skirt and stocking or choose different fabrics altogether to make this charming project. Eliminate the star-shaped wooden buttons to make a table runner instead of a wall quilt.

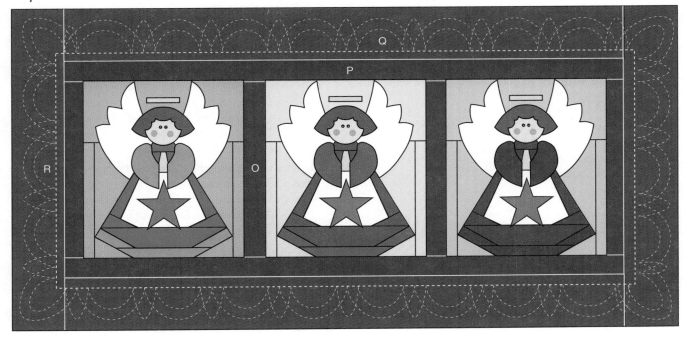

Angel Wall Quilt
Placement Diagram
15" x 32"

Project Specifications

Quilt Size: 15" x 32"
Block Size: 8" x 9"

Fabric & Batting

- 1/8 yard of each of the following: 3 cream background prints, 3 red prints or checks (dresses), 3 red-with-cream ticking-style stripes (aprons) and cream-with-white print (wings)
- 1/4 yard dark green or charcoal print (sashing)
- 1/2 yard brick red print (borders, binding)
- Scraps of the following: tan (hair), skin tone (face, hands), gold/yellow (halo) and 3 green prints or checks (hem, sleeves)
- Backing 19" x 36"
- Batting 19" x 36"

Supplies

- 1/8 yard each fabric stabilizer and light- or medium-weight fusible transfer web
- 3 star-shaped 2 1/4" wooden buttons (painted and drilled per instructions)
- Red crochet cotton (to attach buttons)

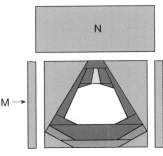

Figure 1
Sew M pieces to sides and N piece to the top of pieced Angel skirt sections.

- All-purpose thread to closely match appliqué fabrics
- 1 spool contrasting quilting thread
- Black and cream acrylic tole paint (for eye details)
- 1 small jar gesso (adds texture to buttons)
- Lichen gray, beige and dark brown acrylic paints (to paint buttons)
- Glossy acrylic spray (for buttons)
- Rose acrylic stencil paint or rose blush (for eyes and face)
- Toothbrush, tapestry needle and stencil brush

Instructions

1. Complete piecing three Angel skirt sections as in steps 1 and 2 for tree skirt using fabrics listed and referring to the photo for color placement.

2. Cut two M strips from each of the three cream background prints 1 1/4" x 6 1/4" and one N strip 3 3/4" x 8 1/2".

3. Cut four strips dark green 1 1/2" x 9 1/2" for O and two strips 1 1/2" x 28 1/2" for P.

4. Cut two strips brick red 2 1/2" x 28 1/2" for Q and two strips 2 1/2" x 15 1/2" for R.

5. Referring to Figure 1, stitch one matching M strip to side edges of Angel blocks and N strip to top edge of blocks; press.

6. Appliqué angel pieces as in steps 1 and 2 for tree skirt, omitting apron hearts. Complete eye and cheek painted details as directed in step 1 in Finishing section.

7. Referring to the Placement Diagram, join blocks with O strips, starting and ending with an O strip; press seams toward O's.

8. Sew a P strip to the top and bottom. Sew a Q strip to the top and bottom; press seams toward strips. Sew R strips to sides; press seams toward strips to finish top.

9. Transfer the Arch and Spear quilting design to border strips Q and R, beginning at corners and connecting the repeat in the center. Mark 1/4" echo lines into background around Angel figure and transfer arch lines below wings as shown on Stocking pattern on pages 14 and 15.

10. Sandwich batting between the completed and marked top and the prepared backing piece. Pin or baste layers together to hold flat for quilting. Quilt on marked lines and in the ditch of sashing and border strip seams.

11. When quilting is complete, trim edges even. Cut and prepare 2 1/2 yards brick red double-fold binding as directed under Finishing, steps 6 and 7 on page 5. Apply binding, folding beginning raw edge under for a clean finish.

12. Drill two small holes in each wooden star; use the stencil brush to apply gesso in an up-and-down motion to create a rough surface texture resembling stoneware. When dry, repeat for second coat. Apply two coats of lichen gray. Lightly apply one coat of beige with a stencil brush until most, but not all, of the gray is covered for a mottled effect.

13. Lightly spatter dark brown over painted stars using an old toothbrush, pulling bristles back and releasing repeatedly. When dry, spray with glossy acrylic.

14. Thread red crochet cotton onto tapestry needle; attach button in place below Angel hands with knot and bow.

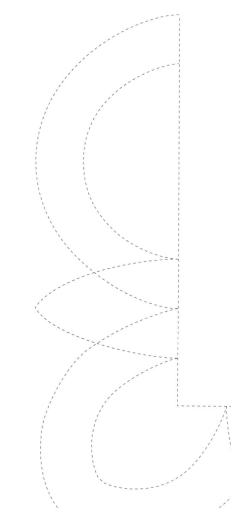

Arch & Spear Quilting Design

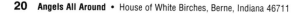

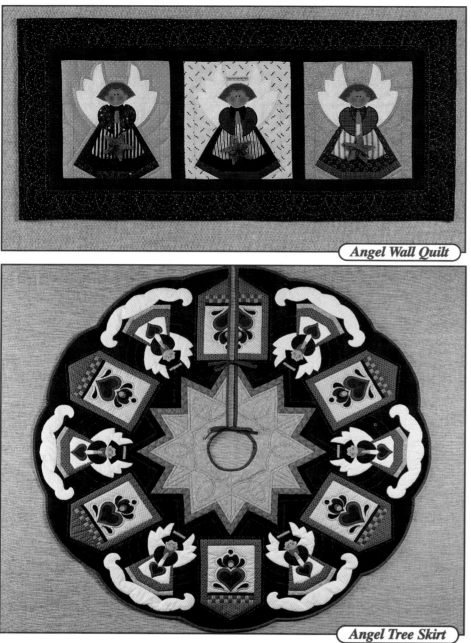

Angel Wall Quilt

Angel Stocking

Angel Tree Skirt

Angel Tree Skirt Detail

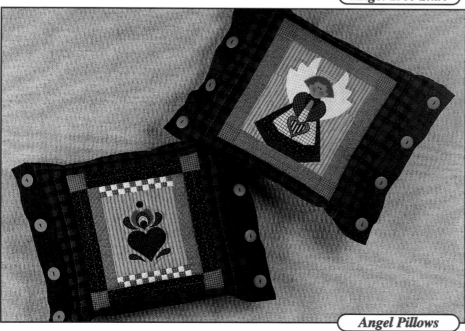

Angel Pillows